CONTEMPORARY ISSUES

DEVELOPING HEALTH and FITNESS Be Your Best!

Girl Scouts of the U.S.A.
420 Fifth Avenue
New York, N.Y. 10018

GIRL SCOUTS OF THE U.S.A.

B. LaRae Orullian, *President*
Mary Rose Main, *National Executive Director*

Inquiries related to *Developing Health and Fitness: Be Your Best!* should be directed to Program, Girl Scouts of the U.S.A., 420 Fifth Avenue, New York, N.Y. 10018.

Credits

Author:	Toni Eubanks
Contributors:	Chris Bergerson
	Joan W. Fincutter
	Sharon Woods Hussey
Editor:	Susan Eno
Design:	Antler & Baldwin, Inc.

First Impression 1992

Printed in the United States of America
ISBN 0-88441-473-6
10 9 8 7 6 5 4 3 2

CONTENTS

INTRODUCTION

Physical and mental wellness is promoted throughout the Girl Scout program at every age level. It is part of our concern for the development of the total girl, and is a necessary component of our program emphases for girls: to develop self-potential, relate to others well, develop values, and contribute to society. When children are attuned to good health and fitness habits, they have a better chance of developing a higher level of self-esteem, a necessary attribute for handling peer pressure and avoiding substance abuse.

WHAT THE STATISTICS SAY

Today's American children are more overweight and less physically active than in previous generations, partly as a result of their less active pastimes such as video games and television viewing as well as their consumption of junk food. Note the following facts:*

■ A majority of all Americans—children included—weigh at least ten pounds more than their desirable weight.

■ Over half of all American children between the ages of six and 16 flunk the minimum fitness test, yet only a small minority of European children fail to pass.

■ A majority of American teenagers get less than half their quota of vitamin C.

■ Pressure from society and peers has resulted in children as young as eight years old going on fad diets and becoming susceptible to eating disorders such as anorexia and bulimia. This problem particularly affects girls.

*Robert K. Cooper, "Planning for Health," *Health and Fitness Excellence* (Kaiser Foundation Health Plan of New York).

CHANGING VIEWS ON HEALTH

Americans are changing in the way they think about health and fitness. We now know that achieving a state of fitness and well-being will improve our resistance to disease and injury, and enable us to live longer, healthier lives. We are also beginning to apply recent findings about the effects of smoking, poor nutrition, and lack of exercise on our bodies. Today, more people are aware that their health is affected by the personal choices they make during their lifetime.

Our objective is to change unhealthy and careless habits into conscious and healthy ones. This book will help you work with girls to establish lifelong good habits of caring for the health of their bodies and minds. It offers girls a progressive Girl Scout fitness plan that they can adapt to their individual needs and interests. These good habits established early in life should continue as girls grow into adulthood. The plan is also adaptable for adults so that Girl Scout leaders can be health and fitness role models for their girls.

Planning a regular, balanced health and fitness plan does not depend on investing money in equipment, health club memberships, videotapes, or trying diet after diet. Basic knowledge and awareness about good health principles and the self-discipline and commitment to follow them are the ingredients for a successful, long-term program.

HOW TO USE THIS BOOK

Developing Health and Fitness: Be Your Best! presents a comprehensive fitness plan for girl and adult participation. Establishing healthy habits is an important objective of this plan, and the activities presented here should make it fun and relatively easy for girls and adults to get involved.

The six components of this health and fitness plan—nutrition, physical fitness, reducing stress, avoiding substance abuse, looking your best, and recognizing environmental factors that affect health—are developed in chapter form. Each chapter contains information and general activities that can be adapted to the age levels, abilities, and interests of girls and adults. For a balanced program, girls should participate in as many activities as possible from each of the six components, with a commitment to continue working on each component as part of their new, healthier lifestyle.

Each chapter ends with a bibliography related to the topic covered. Finally, there is a glossary of terms used in the book and a resource list of health-related organizations.

THE BE YOUR BEST PATCH

After completing several activities from each chapter of this book, all participating girls, Daisy through Senior Girl Scouts, may receive the related participation patch, Be Your Best. This represents the girls' effort and fun while working on the health and fitness activities.

Chapter 1

GOOD NUTRITION, THE FIRST COMPONENT OF A HEALTH AND FITNESS PLAN

Nutrition is an essential component for any fitness plan. The key to good nutrition is to eat a varied diet of fresh foods that are high in complex carbohydrates and fiber, and low in fat, cholesterol, sugar, and salt. Most people habitually select their foods from a limited variety even though they may have a wide variety of fruits, vegetables, and grains from which to choose.

This chapter introduces six steps to healthier eating. The foods described require little preparation and offer a variety of tastes, colors, and textures. The recipes are easy enough and fun for children to try.

SIX STEPS TO HEALTHIER EATING

Step 1: Plan a Balanced Diet.

The American Heart Association recommends the following foods and servings:

Food	Daily Servings
Lean meat, fish, poultry	2
Pasta, rice, beans, and/or starchy vegetables (i.e., corn, potatoes), cereals, and bread	6 or more
Vegetables and fruits	5 or more
Milk products: milk, cheese, yogurt	2 for adults 3–4 for children
Eggs with yolk Egg whites	3–4 a week Unlimited
Fats and oils: mayonnaise, peanut butter, seeds, nuts, olives, avocado, vegetable oil, margarine	No more than, 5–8 teaspoons, or 10 olives, or 3 tsp. seeds/ nuts

3

Step 2: Increase the Amount of Fiber in Your Diet.

Fiber comes from the cell walls of plants: from fruits and vegetables such as apples, grapes, beans, peas, and nuts, and from cereal grains such as wheat, oats, and barley. Some other popular foods that contain fiber are apples, grapes, citrus fruits, potatoes, squash, and oatmeal. Animal foods like meat, fish, eggs, and milk do not contain fiber.

Dried Fruit Snacks

Dried fruit is an excellent way to snack and get fiber as well. Try mixes of foods that have already been dried and chopped, such as raisins and apricots. Add nuts and grains to make your own "trail mix." Or dry your own fruit. Apples and pears can be dried in a low-heated oven.

Fiber in the diet has many benefits. It aids the digestive system and there is some indication that it helps prevent heart disease and colon cancer. Recent findings have also shown that fiber can influence the type of fats in the blood, and its presence in the diet helps protect against heart disease. Research also shows that fiber may play a beneficial role in helping the body maintain healthy cholesterol levels.

The typical American diet is high in animal products and low in plant food. The plant food that is found in the American diet is often highly processed, which robs the food of much of its fiber. To maintain a fiber-rich diet, one should eat natural, unprocessed fruit and vegetables raw or slightly cooked and with the skin whenever possible. One should select whole grain breads such as wheat, and avoid highly processed convenience foods made with artificial additives and refined ingredients.

It is the processing of plant food that robs it of its fiber. Using flour as an example, fiber is found in the outer coating of the grain from which it is made. During the milling process that creates white flour, the outer covering of the grain is removed and the flour is "bleached" white. This process decreases fiber. When the product is "enriched" or fortified, vitamins and minerals that once existed naturally are added. Many modern methods of refining foods also alter them with preservatives, flavorings, sweeteners, and colorings, affecting their nutritional value. Whenever possible, it is best to eat plant foods that are fresh and natural.

The USDA's Guide to Daily Food Choices

The U.S. Department of Agriculture has recently revised its basic nutrition guide and developed a new, pyramid-shaped food chart (see next page). The new nutrition guide will appear in magazines, textbooks, and government brochures as a guideline for how to build a healthy diet. It effectively shows what proportion each food group should have in the daily diet. Notice, for example, that the bread, cereal, rice, and pasta group followed by vegetables and fruits make up over 50 percent of a healthy diet.

Fiber in Grains

Grains are the hard seeds or fruits of plants. They are storehouses of the nutrients that produce future plants. Wheat, oats, barley, corn, and rice are some edible grains. Grains are important sources of protein and minerals in addition to fiber.

Cereal, a favorite breakfast food, is one of our biggest sources of fiber. Selecting whole grain unprocessed cereals is a good way of obtaining fiber in your diet. Since the climate and soil of a region determine which grain grows best, certain foods are strongly identified with certain regions of the world. Through recipe collecting, girls can learn which grains are widely used in different countries and cultures. For example, barley flatbread is widely eaten in Scotland, corn tortillas in Mexico, and couscous, a partially refined wheat grain, is a favorite in the Middle East.

Girl Scout leaders can ask girls to bring in a variety of grains for sampling, noticing their differences in color, texture, shape, and taste.

Barley

Barley bread is widely eaten in Scotland, India, and Italy, but Russia is the world's leading barley grower. Over 20 million tons are are produced there each year. Since barley is a sturdy grain, it can be harvested from the Arctic to the Equator, making barley soup a worldwide favorite especially in Russian, American Cajun, and Jewish cuisines.

The Chinese are credited with being the earliest barley eaters, although traces of sun-baked barley have dated back to the Stone Age. A scene depicted on Chinese pottery dating back to 1520 B.C. illustrates the end of famine with hulled barley falling out of the sky and into a peasant's bowl.

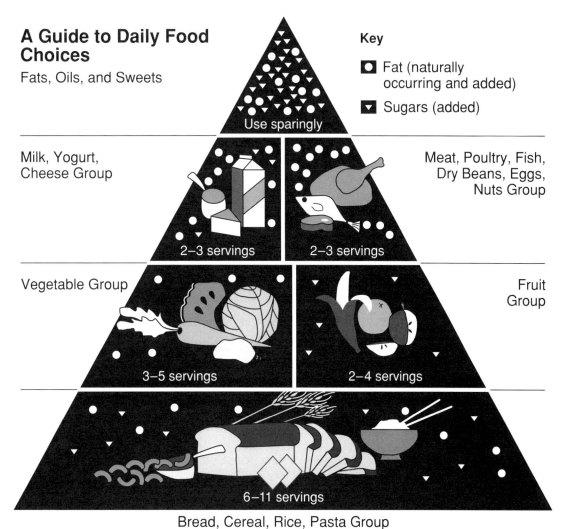

A Guide to Daily Food Choices

Fats, Oils, and Sweets

Key

◨ Fat (naturally occurring and added)

▼ Sugars (added)

Use sparingly

Milk, Yogurt, Cheese Group

2–3 servings

Meat, Poultry, Fish, Dry Beans, Eggs, Nuts Group

2–3 servings

Vegetable Group

3–5 servings

Fruit Group

2–4 servings

6–11 servings

Bread, Cereal, Rice, Pasta Group

The following recipe for barley flatbread produces a thick batter that is best baked in a 12-inch pizza pan.

Scottish Barley Flatbread

3 tbsp. olive oil
1 onion, chopped
1 clove garlic, minced
1 1/2 cups barley flour
1 1/4 cups milk
1/4 cup water
1 1/4 tbsp. sugar
1/2 tsp. salt

1. Preheat oven to 500 degrees. Heat 1 tbsp. oil in skillet over medium heat.

2. Add onion and garlic; cook about 3 minutes, stirring mixture until golden brown. Remove from heat.

3. Put remaining ingredients in blender, or mix by hand until smooth. Combine with onion and garlic; pour onto a buttered 12-inch pizza pan. Bake 15 minutes. Cut and serve while hot.

Bran

Bran is the tough outer covering of a grain, usually wheat or oat. Bran can be substituted for bread crumbs, and a blender can transform it into a flour-like powder to be used in bread and pancake recipes. It can be sprinkled on yogurt and fruit or used in numerous recipes. Most cookbooks have a recipe for bran muffins.

Corn

Corn is the only grain native to the Americas. It was a very important food crop on both the North and South American continents. Corn was derived from a wild grass called "teosintl" and planted in central Mexico 8,000 years ago. The cornfields of the Aztecs grew to the height and size of small forests, and enemies knew better than to attempt an escape in them. Actual corn was found in New Mexico and dated at 5,500 years old.

The American Indians taught the early immigrants how corn could be baked, boiled, dried, or ground into flour and cornmeal. The entire ear of corn was used; nothing was wasted. The cobs were used to make a jelly, and husks were woven into baskets and mats or made into dolls. Called maize by some, corn also has a place in American Indian legends and creation tales, and is a central theme in many rituals.

It has been estimated that by the middle of the twenty-first century, two-thirds of all proteins consumed worldwide will be some form of cornmeal derivative. Girls should enjoy this American Indian maize pudding recipe:

Yellow Maize Pudding

2 1/2 cups corn kernels, cooked (this could be frozen corn or drained canned corn as well as fresh)
1 cup evaporated milk
1/2 cup brown sugar
1 1/2 tsp. vanilla
1 tsp. nutmeg
1/2 tsp. cinnamon
1 tsp. cornstarch
3 tbsp. margarine
2 eggs

1. Preheat oven to 350 degrees.
2. Grease a 9-inch baking pan. Melt margarine in a small pan. Set both pans aside.
3. Add sugar, nutmeg, salt, and cinnamon to corn. Mix well.
4. Slightly beat eggs and stir them into corn mixture. Place over low heat and continue to stir until well heated. Set aside.
5. Dissolve cornstarch in milk; add to corn.
6. Add vanilla and melted margarine.

7. Pour mixture into baking pan and bake at 350 degrees for 45 to 50 minutes.

Mexican Tortillas

2 cups flour
1 cup cornmeal
2 eggs
1/2 tsp. salt
Water to make a thin paste

1. Mix ingredients together.
2. Heat an ungreased griddle.
3. Spread thinly in two- or three-inch cakes.
4. Cook on both sides until done (about 2 minutes).
5. Place tortillas on a plate and fill with your favorite ingredients: chicken, ground beef, sliced tomatoes, grated cheese, etc. (serves 8–10).

Rice

Archeological digs in China unearthed sealed jars filled with rice dating back to 5,000 B.C. (and still edible despite a touch of mildew). Rice, too, is grown around the world in over 7,000 varieties. In Asia, each country grows or prepares it different ways. Rice and barley are referred to in the Koran as "twin sons of heaven."

In India, the earliest dated rice grew in swampy areas and had to be gathered among weeds, leeches, and water snakes. This was the lowliest of all jobs—reserved for slaves or women! Today in India, rice grows on one-third of all tillable land.

Brown rice still has its layer of high-fiber bran, which means that it contains more vitamins and minerals than white rice from which the bran has been removed. This gives it a nutty flavor. Girls can prepare the following recipe for brown rice pudding and compare it to the yellow maize pudding.

Brown Rice Pudding

1 1/4 cups cooked brown rice
2 eggs
2 1/4 tbsp. sugar
1/4 tsp. salt
1/4 tsp. cinnamon
1 tsp. vanilla
2 cups milk
1/2 cup raisins

1. Preheat oven to 350 degrees. Grease a 1-quart baking dish.

2. Scald milk in a small pan.

3. Mix eggs, sugar, cinnamon, and vanilla.

4. Slowly pour hot milk into egg mixture. Mix well.

5. Spread rice in baking dish; sprinkle raisins on top; pour milk mixture over all.

6. Place baking dish in a larger pan; pour hot water into the larger pan, halfway up sides of the baking dish.

7. Bake for 1 hour 15 minutes. Chill.

Legumes

Beans and peas are part of another fiber-rich food family called "legumes." Legumes are plants that bear a pod and split into two halves with edible seeds. Ancient transcripts such as the Bible attribute health and clarity of vision to the eating of legumes. Examples of legumes are green beans, lentils, peas, and kidney beans, but there are hundreds of varieties grown throughout the world. In many countries, beans are an important food staple, often substituted for animal protein. Since legumes grow easily in most parts of the world, they are more available and economical than meat.

The American Indians introduced a dish they called "succotash" to the early colonists. Its major ingredients are lima beans, corn, and green beans, which were referred to as the "three sisters" because in the plains states, the three plants grew in close proximity to each other, and they provided a good nutritional combination.

As America became a more advanced and prosperous country, many people increased their dependency on meat, and stopped living off the land. How many legumes in this short list do you eat, and how often? Chickpeas, black-eyed peas, fava beans, lima beans, navy beans, pinto beans, soybeans, kidney beans, peas, green beans.

Two easy recipes for girls to try:

Lentil-Herb Soup

In a large pot put:
5 cups water
1 cup dry lentils
1 carrot, grated
1 onion, sauteed
1/4 cup parsley, chopped
1/4 cup oil
1/4 tsp. oregano
1/4 tsp. thyme
1 tbsp. garlic powder

Cook over low heat in a covered pot for 15 minutes. Add a can of whole tomatoes. Simmer until lentils are tender, about one hour.

Peachy Punch

5 Ripe peaches, peeled and quartered
8 ounces vanilla yogurt
1/2 cup lowfat milk
1 tbsp. brown sugar
Dash nutmeg (fresh if possible)

1. Place all ingredients in a blender for about 30 seconds, adding ice cubes until thick and well mixed.

2. Pour into glasses and sprinkle an additional dash of nutmeg on top. Enjoy! Serves four.

Step 3: Reduce Sugar.

Most Americans eat too much sugar. In excess, sugar is of little nutritional value. It has been linked to a variety of health problems including elevated levels of blood fat and cholesterol, and hyperactivity in children. Most Americans should cut down on their sugar intake. Since sugar occurs naturally in many fruits and vegetables, consumption of drinks and snacks with a high sugar content should be limited. Most beverages labeled "drink" list water and sugar as their main ingredients (see below). You may be fooled about how much sugar a product contains because sugar may also be listed as glucose, sucrose, corn syrup, fructose, or corn sweeteners on the list of ingredients. A product that lists one or more of these sugars near the top of the list of ingredients probably contains a high quantity of sugar.

A Word About Carbonated Drinks

Carbonated drinks or soda usually contain nothing of nutritional value. Diet sodas may not have large quantities of sugar, but they contain sugar substitutes and have no nutritional value. Many sodas contain caffeine, a drug that may have harmful effects, especially with younger children. A typical 12-ounce can of cola contains 40–70 milligrams of caffeine, nine teaspoons of sugar, and 150 nonnutritional calories. Girls should find more healthy substitutes for soda and other artificial beverages. It is much healthier to drink juice, milk, or just plain water.

Vegetable and Fruit Juices

Juices from fruits and vegetables are very good for the body. They provide concentrated amounts of vitamins and minerals, often more than one would get by eating an average portion of the fruit or vegetable itself. When buying juices, girls can become nutrition conscious by checking labels. Many "fruit drinks" are not truly juice, but water, sugar, and flavorings. Some fruits such as cranberries are quite tart and need sugar for sweetening. For best nutrition, seek out juice that has the fruit or vegetable listed as the main or only ingredient.

With the use of a juicer or a blender, girls can have fun creating healthy beverages like the following fiber- and protein-rich drinks.

Fruit Punches

Experiment with different combinations of pure fruit juices. If you have a blender, you can add whole fruit to a juice base. Some combinations to try are orange juice with strawberries and apple juice with raspberries. Try combinations of three or more fruits!

Banana Milk Shake

2 ripe bananas
3 cups cold milk
1 tsp. vanilla extract

1. Mash bananas with a fork in a bowl or blender.
2. Pour in milk and vanilla; beat in blender or with an egg beater until smooth.
3. Pour into glasses and drink! (serves four)

Pineapple Lemonade

1 cup sugar
1 cup water
1 cup lemon juice (preferably squeezed from fresh lemons)
2 cups chilled pineapple juice
12 pineapple ice cubes (see next recipe, "Fruit Ice Cubes")

1. In small pan, combine sugar and water. Let boil over medium heat for 5 minutes. Then let cool.
2. Mix in lemon and pineapple juices.
3. Place 2 ice cubes into each glass.
4. Fill glasses with pineapple lemonade and drink! (serves six)

Fruit Ice Cubes

Mix juice and mashed fruit for an iced treat. Use 2 1/2 cups juice and 1/2 cup chopped fruit for each 12-cube ice tray. Try this with pineapple, berries, or experiment with combinations.

1. Pour juice in ice tray to about three-fourths full.
2. Add several fruit pieces to each cube.
3. Carefully place ice cube tray in freezer and let freeze. This will take about 4 hours.

Step 4: Reduce Salt.

The body needs only about a quarter of a teaspoon of salt a day, but the average American consumes much more than that amount. Excessive use of salt has been linked to high blood pressure, headaches, and weight gain among other ailments. To give food a fuller flavor while reducing salt, use herbs and spices in cooking instead of salt.

Spices and Herbs

Archaeologists believe that primitive people from at least 50,000 years ago first experienced seasoning when they wrapped their meat in leaves before cooking. Their aim was to protect the food from dirt and ashes, but they soon learned that the leaves gave food a delicious new taste. Spices and herbs were also used for medicinal purposes and to prevent spoiling.

The term "spice" is used to mean any aromatic, natural flavoring made from the dried seeds, buds, fruit, flower, bark, or roots of plants, usually from tropical regions. "Herbs" are aromatic leaves or flowers from plants of temperate climate regions.

Herbs and spices come in a variety of textures, flavors, colors, and smells. Particular herbs and spices are often what give foods from different regions their distinctive tastes. Girls can experience them by bringing in samples to smell, touch, and taste. They can be placed in separate bowls, labeled for sampling. A chart that pictures different herbs and gives their uses can be posted.

Some of the many herbs and spices are: allspice, basil, bay leaves, chervil, chives, dill, lemon balm, marjoram, mint, oregano, sage, thyme, cardamom, cayenne, cinnamon, cloves, cumin, fennel seeds, ginger, nutmeg, paprika, saffron. How many do you use? The following recipe utilizes several different spices.

Spiced Fruit

6–8 cups fresh fruit of choice
4 cups fruit juice (pineapple, orange, peach, or combination)
4 pieces whole fresh ginger
12 whole allspice
12 whole cloves
4 2-inch sticks cinnamon
8 whole cardamom
1 quart low-fat vanilla yogurt

1. Put juice in a pan.
2. Cut ginger into small pieces; add to juice.
3. Add all spices to juice and simmer 15 minutes.
4. Wash fruit and place in dish; pour spiced juice on top.
5. Cover and chill for several hours. Serve with yogurt.

Stuffed Tomatoes

This recipe contains the herb basil, once known as "king of herbs." Basil originated in India, where it was considered a sacred plant and dedicated to the gods. When it became popular in the Mediterranean countries, its reputation changed, and in Greece a sprig of basil was given to someone as a warning that harm would come. Later, in Italy, basil became a symbol of love. It made its way to America in the seventeenth century, where we enjoy it in any tomato recipe.

Stuffed Tomatoes

1 cup cracked wheat
8 large tomatoes
6 small tomatoes
8 small onions, chopped

1 bunch fresh basil
parsley
fresh mint
5 tbsp. olive oil
1 1/2 tbsp. lemon juice
Salt and pepper (optional)
Several washed lettuce leaves

1. Put cracked wheat in a bowl and cover with cold water. Let it stand for one hour.
2. Wash and dry large tomatoes. Cut off their tops and scoop out the pulp. Turn them upside down to drain on a rack.
3. Cut up (or tear up) all herbs into small pieces.
4. Mix the oil, lemon juice, and optional salt and pepper to make a dressing.
5. Scald the small tomatoes for 1 minute; peel; then cut into cubes.
6. Drain the wheat and mix in cubed tomatoes, chopped herbs and onions, and the dressing.
7. Stuff the large tomatoes with the wheat mixture, and arrange them on the lettuce leaves. (serves eight)

Step 5: Reduce Fats.

In the average American diet, more than 40 percent of the total calories still come from fat. This is twice the amount recommended by many experts. About 15 percent of fats in the American diet come from salad dressings, butter, margarine, mayonnaise, and frying oils. Fats in red meat, poultry, and fish account for 30 to 40 percent, and dairy products account for approximately 20 percent.

High-fat diets are linked to several forms of cancer—including cancer of the breast, colon, and ovary—and to cardiovascular diseases and hypertension. It is also believed that high-fat diets cause poor calcium absorption in the body, an important fact for women at risk for osteoporosis.

However, a small amount of dietary fat is important for good health. In the body, fat is stored energy. Different types of fat are found in foods: cholesterol (animal fat), saturated fats, and unsaturated fats. The unsaturated fats help the body use fats properly. Unsaturated fats are oils that are usually liquid at room temperature. They are found in grains, seeds, nuts, and some vegetables, and are used to make oils like peanut oil, corn oil, safflower oil, and olive oil. Some oils like olive and safflower have been found to help lower the LDL cholesterol levels, without lowering the protective HDL cholesterol levels. Saturated fats are found in tropical oils such as coconut and palm, and in animal fats like butter and lard. They can raise the cholesterol level in blood if they become a habitual part of the diet.

Fats, proteins, and carbohydrates are all stored in cells of the body, but the body handles them differently. Proteins are used to build, repair, and maintain tissues, and complex carbohydrates (found in potatoes, pasta, and bread, for example) provide energy. The body also stores excess food in the form of fat. It can store only limited carbohydrate energy, but can easily store fats.

Here are some tips for finding foods that are low in fat:

■ Avoid fried foods. Oil is absorbed in cooking and adds to the fat content.

■ Avoid greasy foods; usually they are greasy because of fats.

■ Look for dairy products that are labeled "skim," "part skim," "lowfat," or "2 percent (or less) fat."

■ Remember, fats come from both plants and animals, but cholesterol is found only in animal products. For example, margarine and butter both contain fat and have about the same amount of calories. However, butter (from animals) has cholesterol; margerine (from plants) does not.

■ Try to reduce the use of fat additives to food. For example, use mustard instead of mayonnaise on sandwiches, spices instead of butter on popcorn. Use salad dressings sparingly. A salad soaked in dressing is no longer a low-calorie food.

■ Nuts of any kind contain fat. Look for dry roasted nuts; they have less fat.

■ Trim the fat from meat and remove the skin from poultry to help reduce the amount of fat in these products.

CHOLESTEROL

Cholesterol is a waxy saturated fat found in all animal products. It is not found in plant products, so when a product such as peanut butter reads "no cholesterol," it doesn't mean that anything special was done to the peanut butter. There never was any cholesterol in it. Our bodies produce cholesterol and use it as a necessary function in the metabolism. But it can build up in the blood vessels and arteries until it obstructs the flow of oxygen and blood. This condition increases the risk of heart disease. Often you will read about two types of cholesterol, high-density lipoproteins (HDLs), sometimes referred to as good cholesterol, or low-density lipoproteins (LDLs), sometimes referred to as bad cholesterol. It is the LDL cholesterol that is a factor in heart disease. High levels of LDL have been associated with the fat buildup in arteries in or near the heart. A high LDL level in the blood increases the risk of heart disease.

HDL cholesterol has been shown to prevent the buildup of fat in the arteries. Very recent research has shown that people with a high HDL level have a greater protection against heart disease than those with a low HDL level.

Some vegetable oils—especially those in tropical plants such as coconut and palm—don't contain cholesterol, but do contain saturated fats that can also raise cholesterol levels in the blood. That's why it is important to avoid saturated fats.

Try substitutes for foods high in fat, sugar, caffeine, or salt:

Food	Substitute
Ice cream	Ice milk; plain yogurt with fruit and a pinch of granola
French fries	Baked potato skins (or sweet potato skins)
Soda	Naturally flavored seltzer water; fruit juices
Potato chips	Freshly popped popcorn
Candy	Dried fruit; granola
Coffee/tea	Herb tea
Salt	Herbal seasonings; onion powder; garlic powder

In a brainstorming session, girls should be able to come up with some substitutes of their own.

Step 6: Drink Lots of Water.

Water is very important for the body. It is not true that drinking water will cause bloating and make you look fatter. Drinking water throughout the day aids bodily processes, including the elimination of waste from the body. Water is also crucial for temperature regulation, circulation, and successful functioning of the immune system. During exercise or in high heat, water is very important to prevent dehydration.

Dehydration

A hot climate and vigorous exercise can result in dehydration, which occurs when you don't take in enough water to replace what is lost through perspiration, respiration, and other body processes. Dehydration reduces blood volume, which may add stress to the heart. During exercise or on very hot days, it can happen quickly. Therefore, you cannot depend on thirst to warn of dehydration. Always remember to drink fluids.

A WORD ABOUT CARBOHYDRATES

For many years people have avoided carbohydrates in the belief that these "starchy" foods add weight. Recent research has shown that the opposite is true: to lose body fat, complex carbohydrates are the important foods to eat. They include vegetables, pasta, breads, legumes, and whole grains.

During the early twentieth century, as much as 50 percent of daily calories were in the form of complex carbohydrates. Today, as is the case in many other affluent countries, Americans are forsaking their healthier eating habits for more expensive animal foods like meat and rich desserts.

UNDERSTANDING FOOD LABELS

The grocery store is one common place where you make important decisions that affect your health. Food labels can help you make those decisions if you read and apply the information on them. The first thing that catches your eye about the front

label of a product is its name and logo. Most manufacturers would like their product to become a household name, so they put considerable time and money into designing a label and developing a logo or slogan. The front label also provides information such as the weight, the form of the product ("condensed" soup or "evaporated" milk), and whether it is packed with water or in syrup. The name and address of the manufacturer, packer, or distributor are also given.

Most of the food products regulated by the Food and Drug Administration (FDA) also have nutrition labels. However, for the time being, nutrition information is voluntary unless a nutrient is added to a food, or the manufacturer makes a nutrition claim on the label—for example, if vitamin C is added or if a product claims to be low fat.

All nutrition labels are set up in the same way. They give the serving size, the number of servings in the container, and a breakdown of the calories, protein, carbohydrates, fat content, and sodium content. The rest of the nutrients listed on the label are the vitamin/mineral percentages of the U.S. Recommended Daily Allowances (RDA). These percentages are established by the National Academy of Sciences, and usually meet the needs of adults.

The ingredients are listed on the label in descending order with the first ingredient listed being the greatest proportion of the product, and so on. This information is important because it tells you what you are eating and in what proportion. For example, sugar goes by many names on a product label, and often several of these forms of sugar are listed on a label: sucrose, fructose, dextrose, lactose, molasses, corn syrup, honey. Coloring or additives are included on this list.

Proposed Regulations on Food Labeling

The Food and Drug Administration has proposed more regulations on food labeling. These regulations will impose uniform serving sizes and spell out more accurate requirements for popular nutrition claims. The changes will go into effect in May 1993.

One of the proposed changes is that nutrition labels contain more information, and that they be standardized. Right now, words like "light" or terms like "lower calories" are often meaningless.

Another proposed change is for more realistic serving sizes. One of the common ways a company improves its product's fat and calorie count is to shrink the serving size on the label. If the product is packaged on two serving quantities, you must double the given information on calories, sodium, and so on. In many cases, the quantity of servings listed is misleading. For example, a bag of popcorn may contain 2 1/2 servings, but the average person consumes it as a single serving. Soon the nutritional information on all labels will reflect serving sizes consumed by an average adult.

The following additional information may also be available soon on labels: saturated fat, fiber, cholesterol and calories from fat, a listing of ingredients by percentage of volume or weight rather than by weight alone, a listing of flavors, colors, and spices.

The FDA has predicted that the healthier eating patterns which will result from the new food labels will save over $100 billion in health care costs over the next 20 years. But the public will have to learn how to read and use the information given on the new food labels.

ACTIVITIES FOR GIRLS

1. Many healthy ethnic dishes are built around grains, herbs, and carbohydrates. Collect healthy whole-food recipes from different cultures that meet the five steps for healthy eating. Have a recipe meeting where you all read through the recipes and select the ones you would like to try. The recipes that come with pictures of the dish (as in magazines) will be most enjoyable to read through. Look for the following ingredients from these cultures (this is just a sampling): Mexican, vegetable-bean burritos; West Indian, peas and rice; African, yams; Irish, potatoes; Italian, pastas; Chinese, stir-fried vegetables.

2. Make a calorie/nutrition composition chart of your favorite foods. Include caloric, fat, sodium, and calcium content along with protein, iron, and vitamin content (vitamins A, B_1, B_2, C, niacin). In your chart, include unprocessed foods as well as "fast foods" such as hamburgers, cheeseburgers, milk shakes, and French fries.

3. Plan a sample menu for one week. You can concentrate on breakfast, snack, and lunch foods that will be quick and easy to make for yourself.

4. Create blender recipes for nutritious drinks. Use combinations of fruit, milk, yogurt, juice, natural flavorings, and other natural ingredients. See how many different blender recipes you can find or create. How about recipes for healthy drinks that do not use sugar? Have a blender party to try out a variety of recipes.

5. Using empty food containers, in small groups or with a partner, practice deciphering labels for a variety of products. Report back on the information you acquire.

6. Compare several different brands of the same canned food by their nutritional content. How do they compare? Which is the healthiest? How much sugar and water are in each product? What additives does it contain?

7. Be a supermarket sleuth. Find out what form of your favorite foods is the best health and environmental buy. Consider packaging, additives, price, nutritional value, and any other criteria that you feel are important. Try potatoes, bread, and juice for a start (in how many forms are potatoes sold?). You may have a nutritionist or other consultant speak to your group about this.

8. Girls can see how foods are closely connected to special celebrations and holidays. To compare the kinds of foods that different families eat during holiday seasons, have girls bring in a recipe that is traditionally used in their home during a holiday of their choice. Ask them to find out if there is a reason or story behind preparing these certain foods for that holiday. Allow each girl to talk about the food and the family traditions associated with it. Compare the different recipes to see what kinds of foods are eaten.

9. Make a crunchy snack for your troop/ group, or for a Daisy or Brownie Girl Scout troop. Young children can help by washing fruit and vegetables, and blotting them dry with paper towel. Older girls can cut the food up in small slices. Some nutritious foods to use are apples, carrots, celery, cucumbers, raw potatoes, crisp pickles, and unsweetened crunchy cereals. Arrange the prepared foods on a large plate to make a colorful display, and have each girl select a few different pieces. Ask young girls to describe the sound that each food makes. See if they can name other noisy foods. The girls could write poems that involve the sounds of crunching food.

10. Play the alphabet food game with young children. Beginning with A and continuing through the alphabet, ask girls to name as many nutritious foods as they can that begin with each letter (let them know if they name a food that isn't nutritious). For letters for which they cannot name a food (perhaps Q, U, X, V), have them make up the name of a food and draw and color a picture of it. Ask them to tell why their new food is so good for them.

11. Make a healthy food rainbow. With red, green, yellow, purple, orange, and brown construction paper, create a rainbow mural. Have girls use old magazines to cut out foods of each color and attach them to the matching color on the rainbow. Example: Red apples would be attached on the red section of the rainbow. The girls can draw and color foods that they don't find in magazines.

BIBLIOGRAPHY

Bounds, Sarah, *Food for Health and Vitality* (London: Ward Lock Ltd., 1985).

Eisenman, Patricia A., et al., *Coaches Guide to Nutrition and Weight Control*, 2nd ed. (Champaign, Ill.: Leisure Press, 1989).

Ewald, Ellen Buchman, *Recipes for a Small Planet* (New York: Ballantine Books, 1973).

Green, Bert, *The Grains Cookbook* (New York: Workman Publishers, 1988).

Henry, Edna, *Native American Cookbook* (New York: Julian Messner, 1983).

Hess, Mary Abbott, *A Healthy Head Start; A Worry-Free Guide to Feeding Young Children* (New York: Henry Holt & Co., 1990).

Robbins, John, *Diet for a New America* (Walpole, N.H.: Stillpoint Publishing, 1987).

Tharlet, Eve, *The Little Cooks; Recipes from Around the World for Boys and Girls* (New York: UNICEF, 1987).

PHYSICAL EXERCISE, THE SECOND COMPONENT OF A HEALTH AND FITNESS PLAN

Chapter 2

This chapter explores the importance of physical exercise for good health and fitness. It introduces a variety of strategies for girls and adults to increase their level and quality of exercise. Americans of all ages are not as active as they should be, and many are overweight. Overall health means maintaining a healthy body, and there is ample research evidence that physical activity and exercise have both short- and long-term benefits.

SOME STATISTICS ON YOUTH FITNESS

Evidence from national surveys reported in *Health Education* magazine indicates that since the late 1960s, obesity has increased 54 percent for children ages 6–11, and 39 percent for ages 12–17; heredity accounts for only a small number of these cases. Overweight children are more likely to be underexercised than overfed. Heart disease risk factors—including obesity, elevated blood pressure, high cholesterol, and inactivity—are now evident in nearly 40 percent of American children ages 5–8 years old. The longer children remain overweight and physically inactive, the greater the probability that they will be overweight as adolescents and adults.

Lifestyle habits seem to be the major cause of overweight and heart disease risk factors. These habits, especially eating and exercising behaviors, are partially established during childhood; therefore, childhood is when the measures aimed at preventing obesity need to be instituted. Getting Girl Scouts involved in an individual or group physical fitness routine is one way of helping girls become physically fit, and filling the void left by public schools. Enrollment in school physical education classes drops as students become older: 97 percent of children in grades 5 and 6 have physical education classes, but only 50 percent in grades 11 and 12 have them. Also, public school students report spending over 80 percent of their physical activity time outside physical education classes.

Studies have shown a correlation between television viewing and obesity. Statistically, the tendency toward obesity increases for each weekly hour of viewing by 12–17 year olds. Children 6–11 years old watch approximately 25 hours of television every week and see an average of 10,000 food commercials a year.

A DEFINITION OF EXERCISE AND ITS BENEFITS

The term "exercise" is used in the broadest sense to mean "moving around" and "using up stored energy." Exercise doesn't have to be a series of activities and motions that must be adhered to on a rigorous schedule. Often the phrase "no pain, no gain" is used when describing good exercise, but this is not necessarily the case. Studies have shown that something as simple as a brisk thirty-minute walk three to four times a week can improve physical fitness.

There are many benefits to leading a physically active life. Exercise is important for every age. In the young, exercise keeps a growing body on track through adulthood. In adulthood, the long-term benefits of exercise accrue. Physical activity can aid in cardiovascular health and can lower blood pressure. Weight-bearing activities such as walking and running help prevent osteoporosis. Emotionally, the antidepressant effect of exercise is widely accepted. Exercise has also been proven to lower anxiety and stress levels, to improve self-concept, and to positively affect social skills and behavior.

An exercised body works more efficiently. It is stronger and less susceptible to injury and physical stress. And of course, exercise does burn calories. For girls and adults who are overweight, dieting alone is not the answer. It goes hand in hand with physical exercise.

BECOMING MORE ACTIVE

Today's life includes a lot of action, but all too often it's on the television or movie screen. Much of our recreation is devoted to the passive activities of television and movie viewing; VCRs encourage us to be even more inactive. Modern transportation has helped us become more mobile, but now cars, trains, buses, and planes do the work that our feet, legs, and heart used to do. Just adding 15 minutes of physical activity to the day would have benefits for most people and wouldn't require a major change in daily schedules.

This is a good time to introduce a physical fitness plan for girls to participate in routinely. Such a plan can be individualized to meet the needs and interests of each girl. Girls can also be encouraged to begin or continue participating in a sport of their choice that might well become their lifetime sports activity. Leaders can stress that physical fitness activities offer additional social outlets for friends and families to share time together.

Before starting any exercise program or participating in a sport, find out if it's all right for the girls to do it. Have a doctor, health expert, or physical education teacher come to your meeting to talk about good health and fitness habits.

TIPS ON HOW TO BECOME MORE ACTIVE

Most people could improve their physical fitness just by walking and moving around more. Walking exercises major muscle groups, and when done at a brisk pace, is an excellent aerobic exercise in which all ages can participate. Also, walking is far less likely to cause injuries than many other forms of exercise.

■ Find ways to add walking or other physical activity to everyday routines.

■ Think of how regular games can be redesigned to include more physical activity; for example, "Simon Says" can become "Suzy Says" and all the movements can become exercises.

■ Make plans to walk briskly with friends to troop meetings and elsewhere instead of riding in a car.

■ Whenever possible, take the stairs both up and down.

■ One evening each week, instead of watching a television show, go for a brisk walk with a friend or relative, take a bike ride, or participate in another physical fitness activity for 30 minutes or so. Build upon this until you involve yourself in a 30-minute aerobic activity at least three times a week.

■ As future activities are planned with girls, brainstorm ways to add action and activity.

TYPES OF EXERCISES

The following three categories of physical exercise are discussed below: general physical activity, aerobic exercise, and muscle conditioning exercise.

General Physical Activity

This relates to how active you are throughout the course of the day. Do you use stairs instead of elevators? When an errand is a short distance away, do you walk rather than drive or ride? Have you adopted the walking routines suggested in the previous section? The more you move around, the more of a workout you give your body.

You can increase your general physical activity. Plot out your daily schedule and see where you can allocate a portion of time, even minutes here and there, toward improved physical activity. Adults as well as girls can do this type of planning. Instead of sitting down for your entire lunch hour, jog or walk briskly with a buddy around the playground or around the corner. Take a dancercise class during your lunch hour, or start one. There are many opportunities within your daily or weekly schedule to become more physically active. You can create your special routine.

Aerobic Exercise

This type of exercise improves the heart and circulatory system. "Aerobic" means "with oxygen." An aerobic activity is one that involves continuous movement which slowly raises the heart rate and sustains it at its increased rate for at least 15–20 minutes, then slowly brings it down to normal. This is a good workout for the heart. Aerobic exercises don't require speed or strength, but they do put demands on your cardiovascular system. Since this requires healthy lungs and a strong heart, it is recommended that you see a doctor before beginning a rigorous program.

Why are aerobic exercises so important? They strengthen the heart so that it more effectively pumps blood through the circulatory system. This delivers oxygen to all parts of the body. Many people who routinely engage in aerobic exercise have slower, stronger pulses. This indicates that the heart is working more efficiently. A healthy heart can do more work with less effort. Aerobic activities include brisk walking, running, skipping, dancing, skating, jumping rope, bicycling, or any brisk, continuous movement that gradually raises the heart rate.

Muscle Conditioning Exercises

These exercises shape, tone, and strengthen the muscles, enabling you to become stronger and better coordinated. These are the exercises performed repetitively such as sit-ups and leg lifts. One of the benefits of having strong muscles is that they protect the joints from strains and pains; strong abdominal muscles support the lower back, control posture, and flatten the abdomen.

The body contains more than 400 muscles. A good physical fitness program strengthens many different muscle groups. Since muscle weighs more than fat, as girls strengthen their muscles, they may not lose as much weight as desired (if that is their goal), but they may lose inches. Leaders can encourage them to keep a record of their measurements instead of constantly weighing themselves. This will better illustrate where muscle has replaced fat.

As fat is replaced by muscle, there is an increase in the energy the body uses at rest, and a decrease in the calories stored as fat. So, once girls and adults participate in a physical fitness regimen on an ongoing schedule, their bodies will burn energy even when they are not exercising!

TIPS FOR AN EXERCISE PROGRAM

■ Pick activities that are interesting. That way your long-term commitment will be easier.

■ Try to participate in a variety of activities. This is called "cross training"—when you vary your weekly exercise choices to work different muscles, thus developing a more balanced state of fitness. For example, you may bicycle or dance on Monday, swim or play volleyball on Tuesday.

■ Build an exercise regimen gradually. Start short and slow and increase in progressive stages.

■ Check with a doctor if you have or might develop any physical conditions that could be problematic.

SPORTS AND GAMES

Involvement in team or individual sports is an enjoyable way to become physically active while developing skills, coordination, and flexibility. It provides an excellent opportunity for girls to experience individual growth and development in a number of areas. Through sports participation, girls can learn how to work persistently toward long-term goals and learn how to deal with success, defeat, and personal achievement.

Participation in team sports helps girls with their interpersonal and team-building skills. They may learn when it's important to follow the rules and when to become self-assertive. They learn the importance of cooperation and sharing to achieve a common goal. Meeting new and different friends from a variety of backgrounds provides a positive foundation for later social interactions.

MEETING GIRLS' NEEDS

The Women's Sports Foundation reports that in sports participation, girls go through four physical and psychological stages. At each stage, the development of the child as a whole person is more important than her athletic accomplishment.

1. The Interest Stage, where most Daisy and young Brownie Girl Scouts are, focuses on having fun, exploring new opportunities to be active, and learning basic movement skills. Simple movement activities and active games are enough to stimulate interest at this stage.

2. The Industrious Stage, where many older Brownie and Junior Girl Scouts are, begins when girls learn how to compete through sports and how to be an important contributor to a team. This is the stage where girls learn the fundamentals of a new skill, and may be playing competitively with and against boys for the first time. Strong, positive support is important now to maintain girls' interest in physical activity.

3. The Identification Stage, where older Junior and Cadette Girl Scouts may be, occurs when girls begin seeking and establishing their identity, which may conflict with their sports involvement. Sports may not be a high priority at this stage, but adult support and encouragement are. Girls need positive experiences to develop their sports participation beyond the first two stages.

4. The Independence Stage, usually begins with Cadette and continues through Senior Girl Scouts. Again, girls are developing a sense of personal identity, are affected by peer group pressure, and are trying to assert their independence. As schools began encouraging girls to participate in sports more actively and more competitively, the relationship between sports and social status has become more noticeable among girls. Those who have remained involved in sports and physical fitness can observe how their skills have continued to develop.

PHYSICAL FITNESS FOR THE YOUNGER GIRL SCOUT

Daisy and Brownie Girl Scouts can benefit from a physical fitness routine that corresponds to their level of development and that they find exciting. These girls will enjoy team activities as an introduction to the world of physical fitness. Such involvement might lead to a later interest in a sport or an individual fitness endeavor.

Most of the following activities can be done in a circle. Leaders will discover how different children are from one another. Some are physically adept and ready for anything. Some have never had a chance to develop agility and coordination. Some have tremendous endurance, and others don't. With everyone in a circle, girls are not looking at or comparing themselves to anyone else. They will all be looking at the leader, who may or may not be their Girl Scout leader (an older girl or another adult may lead the group).

ACTIVITIES FOR YOUNGER GIRLS

1. Follow the Leader: The leader (girls take turns being leaders) instructs the group to follow her in a series of movements: climbing a ladder, reaching for the sun on tiptoes, moving like a windmill, touching toes (with knees slightly bent), and so on.

2. Letters and Numbers: Have the girls form letters or numbers with their own bodies or with a partner. The leader (a different one this time) can call out the letter or number.

3. Circle Romp: To the beat of music, form a circle and begin marching in place slowly at first, then pick up the pace with more vigorous movements. Move around the circle formation; change movements as the leader calls them out: skipping, hopping, galloping. Vary the music.

4. Jumping Rope to Music: Jumping rope increases coordination, rhythm, and timing while it tones up the circulatory and respiratory systems. There are many variations to try, and girls can make up their own: jump with both feet together, cross arms forward, slightly swing the foot and leg forward as you jump.

5. Dancing: With a partner, make up a dance routine that uses as many body parts and muscles as possible. See *Games for Girl Scouts* for more activities.

6. Make a plan to walk three times a week with someone in your family.

7. Take part in rhythmic gymnastics, regular gymnastics, tumbling, dance, ballet, or folk dancing.

8. Have an instructor come to your Girl Scout meeting and introduce you to various stretching and relaxation methods.

9. Keep a picture diary of all the different things you do in one week: watch television, read, play, walk, eat certain foods, and so on. With the help of your troop leader or a consultant, look at what you do and how you might change some of these habits to help get on the road to being fit.

10. Learn how to dress properly for several different activities (raking leaves, jogging outside, hiking in the country, and so forth). What kinds of shoes, pants, tops, and safety items do you need? What can happen to your body if you don't wear the proper equipment or clothing?

11. Jump on a mini-trampoline to music; invite an experienced adult to help you learn the different kinds of jumps to use. Make up a routine to the music. Share this routine with others.

12. Learn how to roller skate. Develop a course in your neighborhood that you can follow at least three times a week. Be sure to use safety equipment.

SPORTS AND GAMES FOR YOUNGER GIRLS

Children exercise their minds and their bodies through sports and games. They explore how it feels to be the leader or the follower, the attacker or the defender; in this way, they unknowingly prepare themselves for real-life goals and conflicts. Additional benefits of playing games include gaining respect for rules, understanding what it means to be fair, improving concentration and memory, increasing creativity, and improving communication skills. Adults should make sure the game environment is reasonably safe and should try not to intervene unless it is absolutely necessary. Try these favorite games:

Crossing the River

Object: To jump across the "river."

Equipment: Sticks or jump ropes laid out on grass to mark the boundaries of the river.

Directions: Lay markers down about a foot apart to represent the banks of the river. Girls make a running approach to the river, and try to jump across it. If they fall in the river, they're out of the game. On round two, make the river banks wider, increasing the degree of difficulty. The remaining jumpers have to try again. This continues with successive rounds until there is only one player left who has not fallen in the river!

Leapfrog

Object: To jump "leapfrog" over players' backs from starting line to finish faster than the other team.

Directions: Establish a starting line and a finish line that are about 100 feet apart. Form two equal teams and begin with a player from each team squatting down about ten feet from the starting line, head and shoulders tucked in. The other players line up single file at the starting line, behind their stooped teammate.

At the signal, the first player in each team "leapfrogs" over the stooped player, placing her hands on the player's shoulders and vaulting over her, legs apart.

After leapfrogging, each player squats down to be leaped over by the rest, so that the second player leaps over two players, the third leaps over three, and so forth. When all players have been leaped over, the original stooped player leaps over the rest and begins the pattern all over. This continues until one of the team leapfrogs all of its players over the finish line and wins.

Octopus

Object: To avoid being caught by the "octopus."

Directions: One player is the "octopus" who swims around in the ocean and tries to catch all the other players, who are "fish." When the octopus yells, "Cross!" the fish have to try to cross the ocean without getting tagged by the octopus. If they are tagged, they become the octopus's "tentacles" and help her catch the remaining fish. The tentacles can be instructed to be stationary and only move their arms to tag the fish, or they can swim around freely like the octopus for an even more active game.

Bronco Tag

Object: For the chaser to join the other players in forming a "bronco," and for the broncos to elude the chaser.

Directions: You need at least 7–10 players to form at least three groups of broncos and one player as the chaser. Broncos form a single line and join each other at the shoulder. The first player of the bronco is the "head," the last player is the "tail." The broncos twist and turn and gallop around, making sure their tail is away from the chaser. The chaser has to join one of the broncos by getting hold of the waist of the tail player. When she does, the "head" player of the bronco that she has successfully joined becomes the new chaser.

Follow-the-Leader

Object: For all players to follow a difficult course invented by the leader in the play area.

Equipment: There should be plenty of obstacles to jump and climb over, run around and through.

Directions: Players take turns being the leader, who takes the group single-file through the obstacle course (running through tires on the ground, hopping on one foot, climbing, and being as creative as possible without being reckless). After the play area has been covered, the leader brings the group back to the starting position and another person becomes the leader.

Capture the Flag

Object: For one team to cross the center line, capture the other team's flag, and return it to their own side without being caught.

Equipment: Two colored flags and a large playing area with some spots for hiding.

Directions: Girls form two teams of equal size and playing ability. Each team should select a leader. One girl is selected to act as a judge and referee. Mark a center line across the playing area. Locate a jail for each side on the opposing team's territory, an equal distance from the center line, and have each team name a jailer. Each team hides its flag on its side of the playing field. Teammates are flag guards and can stand no closer than three feet from the team flag. As players attempt to "capture" the other team's flag, a girl from the opposite side may be "jailed" if caught outside her territory. The girl tagging must say "caught" three times. To get a teammate out of jail, one of her teammates must run to the jail and tag her, saying "free." Since each team's jail is on the opposing team's territory, a player can be tagged and put into jail while rescuing a teammate. The first team to capture the flag wins, or scores points toward a victory score.

Relay Races

Object: To be the first team to reach the finish line after completing the required motions.

Equipment: See the variations below.

Variation A: Crab Relay

At the signal, players crawl backward on all fours to the finish line, then run back and tag the next player, who performs the same movements.

Variation B: One-Foot Relay

Runners hop to the finish line on one foot, then switch and hop back on the other foot.

Variation C: Water Relay

Each team is given a plastic cup of water. Players must place the cup on their head and jump to the finish line and back, spilling as little water as possible. The team with the most water in its cup at the end of the relay is the winner.

ACTIVITIES FOR JUNIOR, CADETTE, AND SENIOR GIRL SCOUTS

1. Take a trip to the recreation department in your community and observe the different kinds of programs that are offered which might help you to reach your fitness potential. Find out if any of the programs have been adapted for people with disabilities. If so, learn how they were adapted. Then, select one of the programs for yourself, and start participating in it.

2. Ride a bike, jump rope, or skip for 20 minutes at least three times a week. Increase the duration and number of times each week as the exercise gets easier. If you ride a bicycle, try to ride in hilly areas.

3. Use the various badges offered in *Girl Scout Badges and Signs* to help you with your fitness program. The Walking for Fitness badge is an excellent example.

4. Water activities, such as lap swimming, aqua-exercise, competitive swimming, water polo, and synchronized swimming, are excellent activities to try.

5. Keep a personal fitness log of all the activities that you will be doing. This will help you as you need to increase the level and length of activity. You should have a weekly log with the date, activity, duration, and amount of repetitions. Include a bi-weekly section for writing notes on your progress. Girls should also include in their physical fitness log a record of their height, weight, wrist size, body frame size, and so on. The log might look like this:

- body measurements
- weight
- age
- starting date
- what your goals are
- how you will chart your progress
- how you will reach your goals
- evaluation
- who will help
- how you will chart your rewards for attaining levels of achievement

6. Learn to play frisbee. What kind of games can you make up with the frisbee?

7. Start a running program. To make it more fun, learn to vary your pace, distance, and course. Keep this program up for at least a month to see how you like it. You may also want to join the track team offered at school or at your local recreation department.

8. Take part in the President's Council on Physical Fitness and Sport Program. You will need to work with your physical education teacher on this.

9. Locate one of the exercise programs on television that is designed especially for the beginning or intermediate level exerciser. Try participating in the program with the instructor. Invite a friend over to do the program with you.

10. Know the important safety rules and precautions for the activities in which you participate—for example, always wear a bike helmet that fits and wear appropriate clothes and shoes.

11. Take up a sports activity that you might like to cultivate as a lifelong interest. Consider golf, the martial arts, swimming, tennis, racquetball, handball, squash, bowling, cross-country skiing, weight training, rowing. These activities performed as hobbies are also good stress reducers.

12. Develop a 60-minute aerobic exercise program that includes: 5 minutes of warm-ups, 30 minutes of aerobic exercise, 15 minutes of muscle conditioning exercises, 5 minutes of stretching, and 5 minutes of cool-down exercises.

13. Set up a series of all-day hikes that cover a variety of terrains. Plan to take along nutritious snacks, a well-balanced lunch, and plenty of liquids to sustain yourself during this time.

14. Design a T-shirt that relates to your health and fitness project. You may develop a personal slogan with a logo, or decorate a shirt with permanent water paints, embroidery or appliqué work, tie dying, permanent markers, and so on. Wear the shirt while participating in the project.

PHYSICAL FITNESS FOR GIRLS WITH SPECIAL NEEDS

When the Women Sports Foundation members were asked about the major barriers to participation in sports by women, their responses were: (1) lack of involvement and training as children, and (2) too few programs outside of schools. If girls are not encouraged to participate in sports and other physical fitness activities, it is not likely they will readily do so as women. And girls with disabilities are even less likely to be encouraged to participate in sports.

Many girls with disabilities are excused from physical education classes in school when, with some adaptation, they could participate in many activities. Physical fitness activities are very important to this population of girls. Becoming physically active can give girls with disabilities higher self-esteem, relieve stress and boredom, and increase energy and strength—the same benefits that everyone receives from physical activity. Appropriately adapted activities can help girls to better understand and appreciate their own abilities.

Girls who use wheelchairs need special mobility exercises to increase and maintain their muscular endurance and cardiac functioning. For girls who are visually impaired, or who have other physical or mental disabilities, physical activities also improve self-image. This enables girls to acquire a degree of independence and self-sufficiency.

Girl Scout leaders can plan physical fitness programs with girls and their parents or guardians. Leaders should believe in the girls' capabilities and stress their ability, not disability. Leaders could help these girls achieve more self-confidence and acceptance by their peers.

Many outstanding female athletes with disabilities can be used as role models for girls. They have mastered such sports as swimming, soccer, track, skiing, wheelchair basketball, and wheelchair tennis. They have proved that others with similar disabilities can participate, and perhaps excel, in physical activities.

Tips for Effective Planning

These are some ways of accommodating girls with disabilities in a mainstreamed physical fitness program:

1. Adapt rules. Rules can be changed or modified without losing the challenge for others. Examples of rule changes in group sports include:

- Shorter or longer time periods.
- More ways to score points.
- Frequent substitution.

2. Adapt equipment. Existing equipment can be made to accommodate a disability. Some techniques make the equipment larger or more colorful; handles may be lengthened or shortened. There are also recreation-oriented assistive devices that make sports participation easier. Many of these devices are inexpensive. There is a plastic head-float device that supports the head above water, a ball with geodesic-type openings that help the player catch it by getting a hand or finger into the web, an extension-handle racket for the user to reach high and beyond her head, and many more items. (The book *The International Directory of Recreation-Oriented Assistive Device Sources* lists many more; see the bibliography at the end of this chapter.)

3. Vary instructional approaches. Some girls are visual learners and need to see something performed. Others are verbal learners and need a detailed verbal explanation. Some need a demonstration and trial run of the necessary movements. Other instructional approaches include:

■ Allowing practice sessions.
■ Increasing repetition.
■ Simplifying directions.
■ Giving immediate positive feedback.

BECOMING A HEALTH AND FITNESS ROLE MODEL

As a Girl Scout leader, you are one of the most important role models girls will encounter during their developmental years. You can help them develop their self-esteem, and their talents and skills; in fact, you may be the one who helps them identify their talents and skills. To some girls, becoming more physically active and adopting healthy lifestyle habits will come easily and pleasurably. To others, it will be the most challenging and difficult commitment they have faced.

You can become a health and fitness role model for your girls by committing yourself to improving your own health and fitness. As you offer encouragement and support to your girls, allow them to encourage and support you in achieving your goals. This book was developed with the intent of involving adults along with girls in improving their health in the six critical areas discussed in the book. As girls see that you are involved in self-improvement, your enthusiasm will carry over to them.

A growing body of evidence verifies that changing certain health behaviors, even in people over 60, can benefit health and the quality of life. Adopting a regular physical fitness activity, eating well, and quitting smoking are three healthy behaviors that you can begin immediately. Also, you can "adopt" those girls who have particularly difficult health challenges, who are overweight, or have unhealthy habits to overcome. Use the buddy system and stay in touch with them between Girl Scout meetings. They will look to you to help them stay on track, and they will motivate you to remain personally involved. The efforts that all of you make at this beginning stage can easily result in a long-term commitment to better health and fitness.

BIBLIOGRAPHY

Cooper, Robert K., *Health and Fitness Excellence: The Scientific Action Plan* (New York: Houghton Mifflin, 1989).

Girl Scouts of the U.S.A., *Games for Girl Scouts* (New York: GSUSA, 1990).

Hubbard, Betty M., *Entering Adulthood: Moving into Fitness*. A curriculum for grades 9–12 (Network Publications, 1991). P.O. Box 1830, Santa Cruz, Calif. 95061-1830.

Journal of Health Education (American Alliance for Health, Physical Education, Recreation, and Dance). 1900 Association Drive, Reston, Va. 22091.

Maguire, Jack, *Hopscotch, Hangman, Hot Potato & Ha Ha Ha*. A rule book of children's games (New York: Prentice-Hall, 1990).

Rikkers, Renate, *Seniors on the Move* (Champaign, Ill.: Human Kinetics Publishers, 1986).

Shape magazine (Weider Health and Fitness). 6 East 46th Street, 2nd Floor, New York, N.Y. 10017.

Sweetgall, Robert, Robert Neeves, and Roba Whiteley, *Walking Off Weight: The Workbook* (Clayton, Mo.: Creative Walking, Inc., 1989).

Sweetgall, Robert, and Robert Neeves, *Walking for Little Children* (Clayton, Mo.: Creative Walking, Inc., 1987).

White, Evelyn C., *The Black Women's Health Book* (Seattle: Seal Press, 1990). 3131 Western Avenue, Suite 410, Seattle, Wash. 98121.

Wilmore, Jack H., *Sensible Fitness* (Champaign, Ill.: Leisure Press, 1986).

Physical Fitness and People with Disabilities

Cooper, Kenneth, *Kid Fitness: A Complete Shape-Up Program from Birth Through High School* (Bantam Books, 1990). 666 Fifth Avenue, New York, N.Y. 10103.

Danskin, David, and Dorothy Danskin, *Quicki-Mini Stress Management Strategies for You, a Person with a Disability* (Guild Hall Publications). 1716 Poyntz Avenue, P.O. Box 133, Manhattan, Kans., 66502.

Nesbitt, John A., *The International Directory of Recreation-Oriented Assistive Device Sources* (Venice, Calif.: Lifeboat Press, 1986).

U.S. Department of Education, *Directory of National Information Sources on Handicapping Conditions and Related Services* (Washington, D.C.: 1986). Write to Superintendent of Documents, U.S. Government Printing Office, Washington, D.C. 20402.

Chapter 3

REDUCING STRESS, THE THIRD COMPONENT OF A HEALTH AND FITNESS PLAN

Reducing stress is the third important component of a balanced health and fitness program. It is believed that one out of every five children suffers from a mental stress-related problem. Stress is the body's response to demands, both physical and mental, that are made on it. The demands one places on one's body may be positive in nature, such as taking a walk, writing a research paper, or meeting a difficult challenge; or they can be negative. All of the emotions we experience, whether good or bad, are stressful: anxiety, fear, anger as well as joy, love, compassion. In fact, nothing would get accomplished in life, no emotions would be felt without some stress.

Positive stress enables us to work and play and exercise, but negative stress can make us physically and mentally ill. It increases the heart rate. Chronic stress can cause the blood vessels to tighten up and narrow until it is harder for blood to flow through (resulting in an elevated blood pressure). Some research indicates that another effect of stress is on the body's immune system. Stress reduces the body's ability to fight off diseases and infections.

Young people today experience a greater variety and intensity of demands that create stresses which the previous generation never had to face. While stress has always been a part of life, society has changed considerably from even a decade ago; therefore, the stressors are quite different. Consider the following results taken from a survey of 47,000 adolescents administered in 1990 by the Search Institute of Minneapolis, Minnesota:

58 percent spent two hours or more per day alone at home.

40 percent spent three hours or more per day watching TV.

34 percent of girls in grades 10–12 report at least one incident of sexual or physical abuse.

21 percent feel under stress or pressure "most" or "all" of the time.

15 percent experienced sadness or depression
"most" or "all" of the time.

13 percent had attempted suicide one or more
times.

7 percent had a parent with a serious alcohol
or drug problem.

The survey was conducted in American Midwestern communities with a population under 100,000; therefore, these statistics are independent of large inner-city areas. The survey results illustrate how much society has changed from being a relatively safe, stable, and predictable world for children, to becoming an unsafe and unpredictable one. Doctors report that more children are manifesting adult stress-related diseases than ever before. And we are reminded that girls are more likely than boys to experience such stresses as physical abuse and sexual abuse. Severe stress more than doubles their chances of depression and low self-esteem.

STRESS INDICATORS

Although girls may not be able to change everything that is causing them stress, they can learn how to cope with and manage their feelings and behaviors. Sometimes just having trusted friends to talk things over with can help reduce the negative effects of stress.

The following factors contribute to stress in children of all ages. Children as young as three years old have been found to have negative physical and mental reactions to stress.

Lack of Adult Support

Many of today's children have no network of adults—grandparents, aunts, uncles, or neighbors with whom they can interact with daily. From the 1940s to the 1950s, American households went from a majority that included one or more grandparents, to a minority.* For some, relationships with adults at home, at school, or in the community may be weak. This often leaves children to fend for themselves in a difficult, complex world, especially if the

responsibilities of adult work result in children having considerable time at home alone.

Strong relationships with parents and other adults increase young people's ability to handle emotional turmoil, and serve to buffer children from negative peer pressure. However, almost 20 percent of the sixth- to ninth-graders reported that they had not had a ten-minute conversation with one of their parents within the last month.**

Depression/Hopelessness

Even though life expectancy for every other age group in America has increased over the last decade, it has decreased for adolescents. Today, life expectancy for adolescents is lower than it was twenty years ago. Accidents, which are usually alcohol- or drug-related, homicide, and suicide are the top three killers of youth. These are behaviors that many young people assume in response to stress. It has been said that hopeless people are dangerous people, especially to themselves. Young people who have felt hopeless or depressed about their current life or their future, may believe it makes little difference how they behave. They may seek pleasure for the moment. Their reckless behavior comes from a sense of hopelessness.

Suicide is a more far-reaching problem than one would imagine. There are 110 suicide attempts for each death, but these only refer to attempts that require medical attention. Many attempts go unrecorded. Also, the survivors of those who attempt or commit suicide are a group that experiences a higher-than-average number of attempts and deaths themselves. Extra professional help should be given to any child whose family member or friend has attempted suicide.†

Dysfunctional Families

There are many ways a family can be dysfunctional, but basically dysfunction exists when the physical and emotional needs of family members are not being met. Being in a single-parent or female-headed family is not enough to make it dysfunctional. Being poor or living in a foster home does

*In 1980, less than 5 percent, as reported in Search Institute, "The Troubled Journey: A Portrait of 6th-12th Grade Youth" (Minneapolis: Search Institute, 1990).

**Ibid. Refer also to the Contemporary Issues booklet *Caring and Coping: Facing Family Crises* (New York: GSUSA, 1988).
†Refer to the Contemporary Issues booklet *Reaching Out: Preventing Youth Suicide* (New York: GSUSA, 1987).

not automatically mean that the family unit is dysfunctional.

Research shows that between 17 and 20 percent of children have a parent who has a serious problem with alcohol or drugs. An even higher percentage of children have parents who are physically or emotionally absent. In some cases, the oldest child or the only child has to assume adult responsibilities such as caring for younger children, cooking for the family, or even becoming a quasi-parent to the parent. Children in these situations must cope with the stress of acquiring too much adult responsibility, without having their needs met.

Poverty

According to statistics from *The State of America's Children 1991*, put out by the Children's Defense Fund, out of every 100 poor children in America:

41 percent are White (non-Hispanic)

35 percent are African American

28 percent live in suburban areas

27 percent live in rural areas

21 percent are Hispanic

Only a small fraction of poor Americans—those families with an annual income of less than $10,000—fit the common stereotype of poverty rooted in the media's images of inner-city ghettos: Only one in 50 poor children was born to a single, teenage mother on welfare in a central city. Poverty affects children everywhere, and it has spread into the suburbs during the past decade.

Poverty brings its own brand of stress. More American children die each year from the effects of poverty than from traffic accidents and suicide combined. Children in poverty often don't receive proper nutrition or health care. One child in eight has no health insurance, and one in ten has not seen a doctor in the past year. Children in poverty are more likely to become teen parents and school dropouts.

Violence/Unhealthy Environments

According to a recent Senate Judiciary Committee report, the United States is the most violent and self-destructive nation in the industrialized world. Many children grow up surrounded by what is called "the violence of poverty." These are unsafe, harsh environments that may be drug-infested or controlled by teenage gangs. Such areas also have more than their share of environmental pollution from chemical and garbage dumps as well as buildings with exposed asbestos and lead paint.

The growing number of children who frequently witness violent incidents rarely get psychological help afterward. Doctors who work with these children say chronic exposure to violence results in problems including depression, anxiety, behavior problems, and low self-esteem. Some children develop a form of post-traumatic stress disorder and may reenact a violent event in play.

Much of these children's stress comes from just being in the environment where they know people are being hurt, often shot and dying in the streets. They may know other children who have been shot as innocent bystanders, and they may, often rightfully, have fears for their own safety. Children who have been traumatized by violence often draw their image of the future as an environment with monsters. Many psychologists feel that nothing is as important to healing the emotional wounds of these children as the personal attention and interest of an adult.

Homelessness

Homelessness is related to poverty. Being evicted and suddenly losing furniture, clothes, toys, and books overnight, moving constantly from shelter to shelter, is stressful and causes emotional damage. Families sometimes have to break up according to gender. One principal reported that her homeless children worried all day that their mother would be gone when they got home.

Media Images

Young people receive a lot of negative images of society in the media's daily news coverage and television images. Violence is simulated in some cartoons and advertisements, and is definitely found in the movies. This can be very stressful, especially for young children, but it is hard to protect children from the media. Some children internalize the violence; some have nightmares, and some reenact violent scenes with each other in play.

There is also the question as to whether the media images that children see give them an accurate portrayal of women and diverse ethnic groups. For girls, the ideals of how one should look and act as portrayed through visual images are often totally unrealistic.

Racism/Discrimination

Racism and discrimination are not easily eliminated in spite of legislation. Numerous groups in America experience racism in many aspects of their life, particularly in housing, education, and employment. They often have to deal with more subtle forms of racism and discrimination, which they confront almost every day of their life. Ninety-two percent of African Americans and 87 percent of Whites believe that racial prejudice is still common in America. There has been an increase of bias incidents in which people are victimized because of their race, culture, or religion.

There is no doubt that in the United States today, with its broad and diverse population and its history, racism and discrimination are a part of people's lives. Children are constantly gathering information about their world. This information helps them form their beliefs and attitudes, and even more important, their own identity. Much of this information is gathered from family, community, school, friends, books, movies, TV, and other media. Victims of prejudice can develop a faulty belief system the same way children learn to be prejudiced. Withdrawal, self-hatred, and denial of heritage are extreme responses to prejudice that some children have.

School

From the time children are five years old until they are 18, nearly eight hours each weekday are spent in the school environment, yet little attention has been given to the impact of the school experience on children. The "Girl Scouts Survey on the Beliefs and Moral Values of America's Children" revealed that doing well in school was viewed by many children as one of the greatest stresses they face. The demands on the child as "student" are quite similar to the demands on the adult in the work world. Therefore, the techniques girls use for managing stress in the school environment are skills they will likely need for managing stress in most work environments.

The sources of school stress are varied. Girls must contend with several subjects, each with a different teacher (representing a different style, personality, world view, etc.), and usually with a new group of peers in each class (see "Peer Group Culture" below). Children are likely to have several exams or reports due on the same day. There is stress from parental pressure or from one's own inner pressure to excel.

The student's "working conditions" can also contribute to stress. These factors include the physical condition of the building, the class size, and how safe girls feel in the school environment. Common incidents of verbal and physical threats, injury, theft, and vandalism are being reported more frequently in schools, causing them to more closely reflect the outside society. The National Institute of Education reported from their national "safe school" study that within a month in the life of America's high schools, 282,000 students were physically attacked, 112,000 were robbed in situations involving weapons or threats, and 800 students stayed home from school because they were afraid to attend. For girls there is the added problem of sexual harassment.

According to the study "Shortchanging Girls, Shortchanging America" conducted by the American Association of University Women, gender bias is an additional source of stress that girls encounter in the classroom. The report states that gender bias takes direct and indirect forms "with teachers calling on boys more often than girls, encouraging more assertive behavior in boys and giving boys the time and help to solve problems on their own, but simply telling girls the right answers." As more teachers are trained in gender-fair teaching, this problem will diminish.

Peer Group Culture

Adolescents usually want to belong to a peer group even though this is not always a happy experience. Most group members have to be willing to suppress some of their own individuality and conform to the group. Some adolescents have not yet formed a cohesive value system, or haven't developed effective coping skills, making it easier to succumb to peer pressure.

Peer groups are usually formed around specific standards. Popularity and acceptance may be based on good looks, ethnic identity, athletic skills, special talents, and so on. Some girls suffer emotionally because they cannot cope with rejection. This causes considerable stress in their young lives.

Puberty/Relationships

Puberty is a time of physical and emotional change for girls. Their bodies are changing and developing, and they are struggling to establish a new identity. During this time, emotions can change suddenly. Girls may be moody or sullen one day, happy and carefree the next.

Puberty is also a time of experimentation, peer pressure to conform, and acquisition of a sexual identity. It is especially during puberty that girls experience stress in their relationships with others, often with people with whom they previously had pleasant relationships. Family members, teachers, even good friends can become sources of stress. However, one of the most important social stresses girls can experience is the stress of sexuality and relationships with boys.

Establishing a sexual identity and relationships with others can cause feelings of rejection and insecurity. Girls can be faced with important decisions and pressures that they feel unable to handle. They may want to be accepted in their circle of friends, or popular with their peers, but may find that doing so could compromise their values. This struggle itself is an important experience for girls. The lessons learned about self and about others, and the decisions made are all important foundations for girls to use to move forward with their lives. And girls will have to experience a certain amount of stress before emerging on the other side.

Body Image

Today's girls often feel that their self-worth is critically linked to their looks. The ideal look that they strive for is unattainable by the vast majority. For some this quest can become dangerous when compulsive eating and dieting are part of the picture. Today, girls as young as nine go on diets. These sometimes lead to physical and emotional roller coasters (see pages 36–37).

Grown women still find that appearance plays an important role in their lives. Cosmetics is a $9 billion a year industry, and countless dollars are spent on weight-loss programs and gimmicks. Girls and adults need to find healthy outlets for their skills and talents so they can see value in themselves, not just in their looks. Girls can observe their eating habits to determine if they are eating for comfort instead of nutrition, or when they are unhappy or lonely. They can be attentive to the connection between stressful events and their eating habits (current research has even revealed a correlation between sexual abuse and eating problems).

Anorexia nervosa is a disease that occurs when vulnerable adolescent females and young women become obsessed with the importance of thinness. The number of cases of anorexia nervosa have increased since 1960. The vast majority of anorexics are young, white, and come from middle-class or upper-middle-class families. However, as others move up the social and economic ladder, their vulnerability increases.[*]

Research has found that youth who were involved in community service projects or any "helping behavior" on a weekly basis were less likely to report risky behaviors. How girls deal with stress during their adult years is influenced by how they manage stress in their formative years. Although it may appear that the stressors in girls' lives are overwhelming, girls can learn appropriate means of dealing with stress, and Girl Scout leaders are in a good position to help them.

REDUCING STRESS:
THE MIND-BODY CONNECTION

In recent years, we have learned about the correlation between our mental, emotional, and physical health. Medical journals have written about the holistic approach to health care: healing the total person instead of treating physical aliments in isolation. An increasing number of medical professionals discuss proper diet, exercise, vitamin supplements, and stress-reduction techniques for curing illnesses.

---

[*]*Girls are Great: Growing Up Female* (New York: GSUSA, 1987), p. 7.

ACTIVITIES FOR GIRLS

Relaxation is a simple but effective method of eliminating tension and offsetting the damaging effects of stress. Activities that are relaxing are good for the mind and the body. There are many simple forms of relaxing and reducing stress: conversations with good friends, involvement in hobbies and fun activities, active involvement in one's religious faith, exercise, enjoying nature and music, even taking a warm bath.

■ Conversation can resolve many stressful feelings. Discuss the importance of sharing feelings with a good friend, and the importance of a sense of humor. Come up with examples of embarrassing or unexpected things that have happened to you, things that seemed tragic at the time, but that you can now see some humor in. Turn one meeting into a ''joke jamboree'' where everyone comes prepared to make the group laugh by telling jokes, riddles, humorous stories, or singing funny songs.

■ Brainstorm relaxing activities to enjoy. Gentle stretching exercises done to music can be very relaxing. The sounds of nature, whether real or recorded, can also be relaxing. There are recordings of waterfalls, rainstorms, and the ocean that bring about peaceful feelings. Bird watching, writing personal feelings in a journal, putting together a stamp collection, playing an instrument can all be relaxing activities. Select at least one activity to participate in three or more times per week.

■ A lot of inner strength comes from religious faith and spiritual beliefs. Become involved in your religious faith and speak to your religious leaders about youth programs in which you can participate. You can work with an organized youth group, participate in a study group, or start a youth group that has a focus such as religious study or charity. You may want to work on religious recognitions for Girl Scouts.* Describe your contribution to the group.

■ Draw pictures or make a collage of your future plans, hopes, and dreams. Use favorite poems, quotations, or sayings. Explain your collage to others. Collectively the total group can create a montage of all of the collages, and display it during a reception or ceremony.

■ One of the greatest pressures on girls is time. Invite a consultant, perhaps a parent or business person, to discuss the usefulness of time management. Make notes of the tips she offers. Practice time management by budgeting your time for one day or one week. First make a priority list of things to do, with the first item on the list as the most important task. Then break the large tasks down into smaller tasks and set a timetable estimating the length of time necessary to perform each task. Create a chart with these categories: task, time needed to accomplish task, who will help, material needed. Practice making and using a time management chart for a Girl Scout project.

■ In small groups girls should plan a skit based on a conflict or an event that one of them experienced recently. They can present it to the total group and discuss the outcome. Following the discussion, the group may want to test alternative endings to the skit.

■ Select music that relaxes and relieves stress— music that can be used to study by, to vent your anger, to relieve depression, and so forth. Select different types of music such as country western, classical, rock, jazz, popular. Bring your selections to listen to at your Girl Scout meeting.

■ Explore your feelings toward people of different ethnic groups and races. Begin by making a list of what you believe about people of other races, both negative and positive beliefs. In a group discussion, or privately in a journal, answer why you have the beliefs that you listed. Finally, list the evidence (proofs, facts) that you use to support each belief.

■ Develop an assistantship project that will enable you to help others. Some possibilities are holding a tutoring clinic in several subjects, reading stories to preschoolers, or helping younger Girl Scouts with their badge, patch, or handbook activities.

■ Read a biography of someone from a racial/ ethnic group different from your own. Share the book with family or friends.

*See *Cadette and Senior Girl Scout Handbook* (New York: GSUSA, 1987), pp. 149–151.

■ Write a play on the subject of racism and discrimination.

■ Participate in this muscle and body relaxation exercise. Select a leader. Get into a comfortable position, perhaps on a cushion on the floor. Wiggle until you feel physically relaxed. Then, the designated leader tells you to close your eyes and follow her verbal instructions for relaxing each part of the body. Starting with the toes and moving up to each body part, the leader instructs you to: "Tighten your toes. Now relax them. Feel your toes totally relaxed." She repeats the instruction by telling you to do the same thing for your legs, knees, stomach, etc., working your way up the body to your head.

■ Stretch a long piece of yarn or string partway along one side of the room, and attach to two chairs. Tell young Girl Scouts to draw a picture of something that makes them feel happy. Encourage them to use their favorite colors. When they finish, let them take turns clipping their pictures to the yarn, describing them, and explaining why the pictures make them happy. Each week they can add a picture to the line.

■ Cut out magazine pictures of young children with different expressions on their faces. Ask girls how they think each child is feeling based on her facial expression, and what they think will happen next in the picture.

■ Select music of all types, moods, and tempos. If possible, tape the different musical selections so that the mood and tempo change every two or three minutes. Ask girls to move or dance around the room according to how the music makes them feel. Talk about their movement experience; ask them what they liked the most, the least, and how they felt.

■ Discuss with girls situations that make them feel happy, sad, angry, or afraid. Have them create masks that express these feelings. They can use paper plates, crayons, yarn, pieces of fabric, or other material. Handles can be made by stapling cardboard strips to the bottom of their masks. On one side girls can draw or paint their happy face, on the other side, their sad face. When they finish, ask them to hold up the side that shows how they feel now. If they want, they can talk about their feelings.

■ For quiet time, select poems that are relaxing and read them to younger girls.

STRESS-MANAGEMENT EXERCISES FOR GIRLS WITH DISABILITIES

A large group of youth with disabilities need to be given viable expectations and challenges. Too frequently young people with disabilities are not expected to assume normal societal roles: baby-sitting a younger sibling, working at the local fast food restaurant. Often they do not have access to exercise, so they tend to get overweight. They too can become frustrated and depressed because they can't work off their tensions. They may become bored, or become risk takers like other youth their age, and turn to cigarettes, alcohol, or drugs. Dealing with depression is a very important issue for these young people.

*Quicki-Mini Stress-Management Strategies for You a Person with a Disability,** by David G. Danskin and Dorothy V. Danskin, is a good resource for stress-management techniques for persons with disabilities (and even for those who have no disabilities). One exercise has participants tie bright-colored yarn with a strip of velcro onto the clock, refrigerator door, phone, bed lamp, their assistive device, or backpack. To this yarn they can attach smiling faces, jokes and cartoons, pictures and words from magazines reminding them to "relax" or "stretch." The book also offers relaxation strategies such as breathing techniques and stretching exercises, and there is a section of suggestions for people with specific disabilities.

BIBLIOGRAPHY

American Association of University Women, *Shortchanging Girls, Shortchanging America: A Call to Action* (AAUW, 1991). 1111 Sixteenth Street N.W., Washington, D.C. 20036-4873.

*Guild Hall Publications, P.O. Box 133, 1716 Poyntz Ave., Manhattan, Kans. 66502

Elkind, David, *All Grown Up and No Place to Go* (Reading, Mass.: Addison-Wesley, 1984).

Girl Scouts of the U.S.A., *Caring and Coping: Facing Family Crises.* Contemporary Issues booklet (New York: GSUSA, 1988).

Girl Scouts of the U.S.A., *Reaching Out: Preventing Youth Suicide.* Contemporary Issues booklet (New York: GSUSA, 1988).

Girl Scouts of the U.S.A., *Valuing Differences: Pluralism* Contemporary Issues booklet (New York: GSUSA, 1990).

Jacobs, Marjorie, *Building a Positive Self-Concept: 113 Activities for Adolescents* (J. Weston, Walch, 1988). P.O. Box 658, Portland, Maine 04104-0658.

Kreidler, William J., *Teaching Concepts of Peace and Conflict* (Cambridge, Mass.: Educators for Social Responsibility, 1990). 23 Garden Street, Cambridge, Mass. 02138.

Salzman, Marian, and Teresa Reisgies, *150 Ways Teens Can Make a Difference: A Handbook for Action* (Princeton, N.J.: Peterson's Guides, 1991).

Search Institute, "The Troubled Journey: A Portrait of 6th–12th Grade Youth" (Minneapolis, Minn.: Search Institute, 1990). 122 W. Franklin Avenue, Suite 525, Minneapolis, Minn. 55404.

Chapter 4

AVOIDING HARMFUL SUBSTANCES, THE FOURTH COMPONENT OF A HEALTH AND FITNESS PLAN

Substance abuse is a problem that confronts many girls as they begin to deal with the pressures of living in today's world. This dilemma not only includes illegal drugs such as marijuana and cocaine, but misused prescription drugs, alcohol, tobacco, and substances like paint and glue that are inhaled. Drug abuse can be particularly harmful to growing and developing minds and bodies, and may have a lifelong impact even if abusive behavior is stopped.

Drugs affect the four areas of growth: physical growth, or sexual development, which begins during the adolescent years; intellectual growth, which is the ability to take in information and use ideas; and emotional growth, which relates to feelings and relationships with others. One can look upon drugs as invading enemies that cause the developing body to constantly protect itself instead of continuing its normal function of growth.

ADOLESCENCE AND SUBSTANCE ABUSE

Statistics in a report titled "Drug Use Among American High School Students, College Students, and Other Young Adults"* state that 90 percent of high school seniors have used alcohol by their senior year, and 51 percent have used illegal drugs. A majority of those using illegal drugs reported that marijuana was the drug they used, but 10 percent reported using cocaine.

Many children begin their alcohol and drug use at a young age. Forty-five percent of those students who used marijuana smoked for the first time by age 11, and children start using alcohol regularly in junior high school. *The Weekly Reader*, a national children's magazine, reports that one-third of the fourth-graders questioned felt that drinking beer, wine, or other liquor is a big problem among their peers. They reported being aware that some children in the fifth and sixth grades also smoke cigarettes, smoke marijuana, and sniff glue. This shows that ed-

*U.S. Department of Health and Human Services, 1989.

ucational preventive programs should start in the early elementary years.

Alcohol

Alcohol is the most abused drug among youth, followed by tobacco. By the time they reach twelfth grade, most alcohol abusers drink alcohol at least once a week. A majority of them report that they have been drunk at least once. Many teenagers say their drinking habit has created problems with school, friends, or police. Often alcohol is readily accessible at home or in the homes of friends.

American society tends to view alcohol as separate from other drugs. However, it is a depressant that is legal, cheap, and not difficult for minors to get. Intoxication can last anywhere from one to 12 hours depending on the quantity consumed, the amount of food in the stomach, body size, and how fast it is consumed.

Alcohol affects the digestive system, especially the liver, which must process 90 percent of it. Alcohol also affects the circulatory system, in which blood vessels enlarge; and the brain, where alcohol depresses speech, memory, vision, judgment, and reflexes.

Beer and wine are as harmful as hard liquor, yet a recent survey showed only 25 percent of 7th-through 12th-graders considered wine coolers to be a drug. Two-thirds of the older children reported feeling pressure to try these sweet-tasting alcoholic beverages. For teenagers, the most life-threatening consequence of alcohol abuse is when they drink and drive.

Cigarette Smoke

Smoking is linked to cancer malignancies in the lungs, larynx, esophagus, bladder, and cervix. It is also linked to heart attacks, strokes, and fetal abnormalities in pregnant smokers. Smoking has declined among all major age, race, and sex groups *except for young females.* More women are smoking heavily and starting to smoke earlier than they did 20 years ago. Each day approximately 1,600 American teenage girls light up for the first time. As lung cancer has decreased in men, it has risen in women. A positive turning point for girls and adult women is that lung cancer is now being discussed as a women's issue.

There has recently been increased citizen action against cigarette companies that target selected populations for extensive advertising. Black communities in particular have seen ad campaigns in which they have been targeted. Many of these communities have organized to successfully fight these efforts to increase cigarette use.

A new study conducted early in 1991 found that no matter what age a person is or how long she has smoked, there are real benefits to reap from giving it up. Even smokers who reach their seventies are likely to live longer if they quit. The study showed that those who smoked doubled their risk of dying from both heart disease and cancer. However, women who quit faced the same cancer death risk as those who never smoked, while men who gave up smoking still had about a 50 percent higher risk.

Passive Smoking

Passive smoking, also called secondhand or involuntary smoking, is the inhalation of smoke produced by another person's cigarette. The Surgeon General's 1986 "Report on Involuntary Smoking" documents the health hazards of involuntary smoking for nonsmokers. Between 500 and 5,000 nonsmokers die annually of lung cancer caused by others' cigarettes. This makes tobacco smoke the nation's most lethal airborne carcinogen.

Passive smoke contains at least as high a concentration of toxic and cancer-causing chemicals as the smoke that is inhaled directly. Much of the nicotine from a smoker's cigarette ends up in the atmosphere. Passive smoking among children of smokers has been found to cause a slower growth of lung volume and a higher incidence of bronchitis, pneumonia, and other respiratory illnesses.

Chewing Tobacco

Chewing tobacco increases the risk of cancer of the mouth, coats the tongue, and stains the teeth. Approximately 5 percent of the 47,000 youths interviewed in a Search Institute survey (see bibliography) reported that they had used chewing tobacco 20 or more times in the last year. It is believed that previous advertisements of athletes and other macho-looking models especially had an effect on impressionable young males.

Amphetamines

These drugs were developed in the 1930s for clinical use to help obese women lose weight. The popular "diet pill" was originally an amphetamine misused by women and overprescribed by doctors. They are often first used by adolescents to cram late at night for an exam, or to pep themselves up before an athletic event.

Amphetamine users deteriorate physically from ulcers, skin disorders, and malnutrition. They may experience brain damage, hallucinations, and paranoia. The body is subjected to cycles of emotional highs and lows that are extremely stressful.

Marijuana

Even occasional smokers can acquire a psychological dependence on marijuana. Girls should know that it can take the body as long as 30 days to rid itself of the drug. Habitual use destroys brain cells and harms short-term memory retention. When the UCLA Medical School studied 229 marijuana smokers, they found that smokers suffered from acute bronchitis, and the large airways in their lungs were harmed. These drug abusers are at high risk of contracting lung cancer from carcinogens.

Cocaine/Crack

Once thought to be relatively harmless, cocaine is now viewed as having many dangers. Cocaine users may suffer from chronic depression, panic attacks, memory loss, hallucinations, and addiction. Long-term physical symptoms include nausea and vomiting, severe headaches, fatigue, cold sweats, and persistently dry throats. There is the risk of contracting skin abscesses, hepatitis, and AIDS when any drug is injected with shared needles.

Crack is a recent form of cocaine, also called "rock." It is cocaine mixed with other nondrug ingredients until it forms a paste. After it hardens, it can be broken into pieces ("rocks") and smoked. These pieces are sold more cheaply than cocaine on the streets, but create a dependency in a much shorter time. Smoking the drug means that it reaches the brain much more quickly, creating an intense high. To recover from dependency on any form of cocaine, the addict has to stop using the drug.

Steroids

These are a group of powerful compounds closely related to the male sex hormone testosterone. They were developed in the 1930s and are prescribed today in a safe form mainly to treat allergies and skin rashes. Athletes began using steroids in the 1950s after they were found to increase muscular strength and performance. Today, young people are trying steroids to accelerate their physical development.

Misuse of steroids can create serious side affects. The liver and the cardiovascular and reproductive systems are most affected. In females, masculine traits can develop along with breast reduction and sterility. Steroids can cause personality changes, and users may have less control over their emotions.

MYTHS AND FACTS

Below are some common myths that young people have concerning alcohol, drugs, and tobacco, followed by the facts.

MYTH: You have to use drugs for a long time before you become addicted to them.

FACT: Many drugs are quickly addictive and immediately have negative effects on the body. They can cause the brain to send wrong signals to the body, causing irregular breathing, heart attack, or even death. This may even happen after the first use.

MYTH: If you smoke marijuana on Saturday, you'll be fine on Monday.

FACT: Marijuana can affect a person's coordination, reflexes, and memory for up to three days after use. It can remain in the body as long as four weeks after use.

MYTH: You have to inject cocaine to become addicted to it.

FACT: Cocaine is addictive whether it is smoked, snorted, or injected.

MYTH: If you get drunk, coffee will sober you up.

FACT: It takes time for alcohol to work its way out of the bloodstream. Only then will you be sober.

MYTH: Drugs relieve stress and relax you.

FACT: Drugs can cause you to ignore your responsibilities and abuse those whom you love. When drugs wear off, your responsibilities are still there and you have hurt yourself and those closest to you. Drugs can make your heart beat faster and blood pressure rise. You may feel sick to your stomach, get a bloody nose, or hallucinate.

MYTH: Marijuana isn't as bad for you as cigarettes.

FACT: Marijuana has more cancer-causing chemicals than tobacco.

MYTH: You can stop using drugs at any time.

FACT: It is not easy to stop using drugs. You may experience withdrawal sickness, and you may have a psychological dependence on drugs that will make it difficult to stop. Most addicts require intensive professional help to quit.

There are two kinds of drug dependency: addiction and habituation. Addiction is a physical dependence on the drug. Some drugs are addictive because their chemical structure locks into the body's chemistry. The addict has a physical need for the drug, a "craving" that can be so strong that the addict needs the drug just to feel normal. The process of addiction can be slow or fast, depending on the drug and the person.

Habituation is a psychological dependence on the drug. It is just as dangerous as addiction, and often harder to recover from.

When first becoming involved with drugs, the user gets the desired high. But after a while, the body builds up a tolerance to the drug and more is needed to get the same high.

SUBSTANCE ABUSE AND OTHER HEALTH PROBLEMS

At what point does drug or alcohol use become abuse? Abuse occurs when the drug is taken regularly and in amounts that make it difficult to function responsibly. Abuse can lead to dependency, which occurs when the user begins to focus her life around getting the drug and staying high. At one time dependency was looked upon as a social disgrace. Now it is considered a disease.

Smoking and heavy alcohol use are factors in the aging and wrinkling of skin. Smoking depletes the body's supply of vitamin C. They both can raise the risk of osteoporosis, which is a bone loss problem common in older women. It can lead to an aching or curved back, or hips and wrists that fracture easily. Although heredity plays a major role in developing osteoporosis, exercise and a diet high in calcium can help strengthen bones and reduce the effects of the disease.

Cigarette smoking, alcohol, and drugs can affect the fetus of a pregnant girl or woman. Such babies can be born with one or more life-threatening symptoms including low birth rate, developmental deformities, brain damage, even drug addiction.

ACTIVITIES FOR GIRLS

1. Organize awareness campaigns about the use of cigarettes and tobacco. Become involved in making schools and extracurricular events smoke-free. Working in small groups, develop anti-smoking posters that tell about the harmful effects of smoking. Display them in public locations on the "Great American Smokeout Day," which usually falls in November. Obtain more information from your local American Cancer Society.

2. Invite a professional to speak to your group on the topic of substance abuse. As a group, think of possible drug awareness activities that you would like to do. Make a list of all your ideas. Talk about each one and come to an agreement about what you will do. Put your plan into action.

3. Talk about some of the different feelings that people have—happy, sad, embarrassed, angry, loved, afraid, jealous, proud, nervous, and so on. Share what makes you feel each emotion. Make masks that express some of these feelings.

4. Discuss the following situations and role-play what you would do if:

- Your best friend tells you that she smokes marijuana.
- The smoke from a stranger's cigarette is bothering you.
- A classmate offers you money to sell a joint.

■ Your cousin offers you a drink of wine.
■ Several family members are drug abusers who mistreat the youngest members of the family.

5. Write a journal entry about some of the things that make you feel good about yourself. Include the things you are proud of—your good qualities, your accomplishments, and things you do well. Share this information with others.

6. Find out about careers in health and counseling. Select one you might be interested in and, if possible, talk to someone who works in that career. Make an informal presentation about the career.

7. Make a drug awareness exhibit for a shopping mall, library, or school to educate others in your community. Display some of this information on poster boards and distribute some as leaflets. Be sure to include information on different types of drugs and their harmful effects, why it is important to say no to drugs, and where to get help if someone is using drugs.

Include in the exhibit a scrapbook of drug- or alcohol-related incidents or accidents formed in part from photos, stories, and headlines cut from the newspaper.

8. Make a drug abuse prevention presentation to younger children. This may include a puppet show, drama, or audiovisual production.

9. Become part of a community self-help hot line, or work toward starting one in your area.

10. Do activities from the Contemporary Issues booklet *Tune In to Well-Being, Say No to Drugs* (see bibliography).

11. Some contemporary songs contain messages that are for or against drugs and alcohol. Select and play some of these songs, and write down their lyrics. Discuss the possible meanings and why artists might choose to sing about these topics.

12. Write a 60-second public service advertisement that is against substance abuse. Act it out and videotape it if possible. Show it to other children and adults.

13. Collect and study two or three ads promoting alcohol or tobacco to learn the image that manufacturers portray to increase sales of their products. For each ad discuss:

■ What image is portrayed (romantic, macho, athletic, glamorous, etc.).
■ Toward whom the ad is directed.
■ What need is being addressed.
■ Whether it is a realistic portrayal of life (why or why not?).
■ What three alternatives could meet the need suggested in the ad?

BIBLIOGRAPHY

Barun, Ken, and Philip Bashe, *How to Keep the Children You Love Off Drugs* (New York: Atlantic Monthly Press, 1988).

Gerne, Patricia J., and Timothy A. Gerne, *Substance Abuse Prevention Activities for Elementary Children* (Englewood Cliffs, N.J.: Prentice-Hall, 1986).

Girl Scouts of the U.S.A., *Tune In to Well-Being, Say No to Drugs: Substance Abuse.* Contemporary Issues booklet (New York: GSUSA, 1985).

Knox, Jean McBee, *Drinking, Driving and Drugs* (New York: Chelsea House Publishers, 1988).

Scott, Sharon, *PPR: Peer Pressure Reversal—How to Say No and Keep Your Friends* (Amherst, Mass.: Human Resource Development Press, 1986).

Search Institute, *The Troubled Journey: A Portrait of 6th–12th Grade Youth* (Minneapolis, Minn.: Search Institute, 1990). 122 West Franklin Avenue, Suite 525, Minneapolis, Minn. 55404).

Chapter 5

LOOKING YOUR BEST, THE FIFTH COMPONENT OF A HEALTH AND FITNESS PLAN

Barbie, the popular doll that so many girls still grow up with, celebrated her thirtieth birthday in 1990. To many people, Barbie represents the American "ideal," the standard of beauty against which all females are tested: the young, blonde, blue-eyed, tall, slender image of feminine perfection. American females of all ages and stations in life have taken themselves through physical, psychological, and financial hardships to try to live up to the Barbie image.

Women more than men are judged on their physical appearance; consequently, a woman's body image influences her acceptance in the world and her self-esteem. Even movie stars and models have to work at meeting the American standard of beauty by altering their body and features. They use cosmetic surgery to straighten noses, lift eyelids, eradicate wrinkles, plump up lips, get rid of fat, add breasts, reduce breasts, etc. A bottle of hair dye turns brunette or gray hair blonde, and colored contact lenses turn dark eyes blue. Even those women who seem to meet the ideal standard of beauty in our society are sometimes victims of that standard themselves. If everybody has to work so hard to achieve even some portion of this standard of beauty, couldn't this indicate that something is wrong?

GROWING UP WITH UNREALISTIC EXPECTATIONS

How is this unrealistic image of beauty perpetuated in our society, and how does it affect each generation of girls? Our attitudes and values are shaped by family and society. Culture is reflected all around us, but especially in our folk tales and fairy tales, in the magazines and billboards we read, the television and movies we watch. The images reflected back at us are the heroines with whom girls identify, heroines who are almost always young, white, and blonde. Internalizing this one standard of beauty often results in young girls developing negative concepts of themselves.

Many girls become dissatisfied with their bodies long before they have figures. The American girl's fear of becoming fat may begin at age seven or eight, and intensify with age. At this early stage, girls have already idealized thinness and become preoccupied with it. Such preoccupation can lead to an unhealthy self-image, to eating disorders such as anorexia nervosa, and to stress (see pp. 34–35).

According to the National Association of Anorexia Nervosa and Associated Disorders, there is a "false conception of the female body that is repeated in a thousand different ways." And young girls buy into the concept much too frequently. Often they are prone to excessive dieting and eating disorders. Another message girls continue to receive in our society is that boys do not like girls who are smarter than they are. The danger in harboring such feelings is that girls will look outward rather than inward for self-esteem.

THE EVER CHANGING CONCEPTS OF BEAUTY

One writer translated Barbie's measurements to fit a real-life woman. What they translate to is this: a real-life Barbie would be 5′6″ with measurements 36″, 18″, 33″; very unrealistic in the real world. Obviously at the time Barbie was produced, the ideal body image for women was large bust, small waist and hips. That was not always the case. When a boyish, flat-chested, less curvy look became popular, women tried to emulate that look. Portraits of women in nineteenth-century Europe and in other cultures reveal an admiration for heavier women. Throughout history, often a couple of times within one generation, the image of the ideal woman's body has changed.

SUGGESTIONS FOR LEADERS

There are many ways leaders can help girls look and be their best. The activities at the end of this chapter will help leaders show girls how to:

■ Focus on what they can realistically do about their appearance, and how they can succeed instead of focusing on unrealistic goals and failure. Help girls to see their best qualities and accentuate them.

Is it their hair, smile, personality? Show girls how to downplay or correct something they can't change. They can exercise for fitness and weight loss (acknowledge that some girls may indeed need to lose some weight). They can also correct bad habits. Emphasize that there is no one ideal of beauty.

■ Turn girls' preoccupation with looks into something more healthy. Show them that beauty is more than outer appearance. It is having a sense of humor, having energy, being a good listener, being helpful, developing their own special interests and abilities. Help girls identify their interests and talents, and encourage girls to develop them. They can spend some time each week, perhaps using troop time, on their individual hobbies and interests. This is one way of developing their unique inner beauty.

■ Acknowledge girls' interest in looking attractive. Boys want to look attractive too. But their self-esteem shouldn't derive just from physical appearance. Cover these ideas in a discussion with girls:

● Movie stars often need other people to sing, dance, and even stand in for them.
● Models sometimes have to be pinned into their garments, because the clothes are so small, so that a certain image can be photographed.
● As stated earlier, professional actresses, performers, and fashion models—on whom we base our ideal—often dye their hair, wear colored contacts, have cosmetic surgery or fat reduction surgery to measure up to an artificial ideal.

■ With the help of a consultant such as a nutritionist or nurse, explain to girls that outer physical beauty is related to the care we give to our inner body. Eating well and drinking lots of water positively affect complexion and hair.

One of the best ways we can help girls is by showing them how to establish healthy habits. Good habits (like bad ones) can follow girls into adulthood. Since the adolescent body is undergoing a major transformation from childhood to adult ("adolescence" means "becoming an adult"), this is a good time for girls to begin a health-conscious routine.

DOCTOR/CLINIC VISITS

Girls should visit their family doctor or clinic for regular appointments. This is an important healthy habit to establish early in life. Scheduling regular health care visits is one way of practicing preventive health care. Girls should learn the value of establishing a positive, ongoing relationship with a doctor or health care worker who will answer their questions and meet their health care needs.

Ideally girls should have regular physical exams once a year. At that time, immunizations can be given if needed. Girls should visit a dentist every six months. Eye exams should be given once a year.

TEETH

Like your entire body, your teeth require good nutrition, good personal habits, and professional health care. Citrus fruits like oranges and grapefruits, and dark green vegetables help promote healthy teeth because they contain vitamin C, an important vitamin for healthy gum tissues. Milk and cheese are also good for teeth because they contain calcium, which is essential to forming strong, healthy teeth.

Plaque

However, most food, even that which is good for you, forms plaque which consists of microscopic bacteria that are present in everyone's mouth. Tartar is formed when plaque is allowed to remain on teeth so long that the calcium minerals from saliva have hardened in it. That is why the best practice is to brush after every meal or snack, but especially to brush before bedtime. Plaque can cause tooth decay.

Flossing

No matter how thoroughly you brush your teeth, your toothbrush cannot reach between all of your teeth and along the gum line. This is where plaque buildup can cause major problems. The best way to remove plaque from these areas is by flossing. Girls should be shown the correct way to floss their teeth.

Check-ups

There is no substitute for regular dental check-ups, which should occur twice a year. If one waits for pain before visiting a dentist, the condition could become more serious. In the early stages, cavities usually do not hurt. During a checkup, the dentist or dental hygienist will check the condition of teeth and gums, and review with girls the proper techniques for daily brushing and flossing. Practicing good dental habits can help prevent tooth decay and possible tooth loss.

CLEANLINESS

Girls, especially during their menstrual cycles and after involvement in sports or exercise, should bathe daily. There are still some old myths circulating about avoiding baths during the menstrual cycle. By contrast, baths or showers are generally encouraged at that time for hygienic reasons.

After puberty, girls need to use a deodorant, usually an antiperspirant, daily. This should be applied only on clean, dry underarms. People with dry skin may elect to use a lotion after bathing. All of these products come in hypoallergenic form for girls with allergies or with sensitive skin.

SKIN

Skin is the body's largest organ. It covers over ten square feet of the average adult's body, and accounts for about 16 percent of total body weight. However, skin is much more than a cover for the body. It is a highly complex organ of protection, sense, elimination, and temperature regulation. Skin keeps out dirt and protects the body from the harmful effects of pollution and weather. It responds to touch, heat, cold, mood, music; to whatever we put inside our bodies, such as food or medicine; and to whatever we put on our skin—lotion, perfume, even jewelry.

Most people are concerned with the surface appearance of skin, but skin is a multilayered system. The appearance and texture of skin are determined by many factors:

- Heredity.
- Diet and lifestyle.
- Stress.
- Environmental conditions: pollution, wind, humidity, and sun (see Chapter 6).

A poor diet of "junk food" and sugar-laden snacks often has a detrimental affect on skin. There are healthy substitutes that girls may agree to switch to (see p. 10).

ACNE

During adolescence, hormones change and oil glands may overreact. As skin tissue, particularly around the body's hair follicles, readjusts, bacteria can grow and produce a plug. This bacteria-infected plug blocks the oil or hair canals and produces whiteheads, blackheads, pimples, or acne.

Heredity, poor diet, improper cleansing of the skin, lack of exercise, inadequate sleep, and stress can all contribute to acne. To minimize outbreaks, girls can:

- Remove makeup before exercising so that it won't block pores.
- Supply the body with proper nutrition and rest (see the chapters on good nutrition and stress reduction).
- Gently cleanse face and hands after exercising.
- See a doctor if the acne persists.

HAIR

Hair is made up of dead cells that are produced by living cells under the skin. The state of health of one's hair can reflect the health of her body (the exception is if hair has been affected by a chemical process). Every girl's hair has its own assets and its own problems.

Diet, illness, and drugs can change the body's metabolism enough to slow down hair growth and luster. Excessive use of curling irons, electric curlers, and blow dryers will dry out the hair and scalp. Girls should limit the use of these products.

The type of hair—fine, medium, coarse, straight, wavy, curly, dry, or oily—will affect the kind of care it needs. Girls can learn to take advantage of what they have. Often girls strive to dramatically alter their hair, which may end up damaging it.

ACTIVITIES FOR GIRLS

1. Make your own beauty products. Select a natural cosmetics book that has recipes for creams, astringents, masks, and other beauty items. Many recipes are simple and the ingredients can be found in the grocery store, drugstore, medicine cabinet, or kitchen. The following recipes are examples:

Honey Cleanser

2 tsp. honey
1/3 cup water
4 tbsp. ground orange peel
4 tbsp. vinegar

Mix all products together to create a homemade cleanser for any type of skin.

Oatmeal Honey Mask

Mix uncooked oatmeal, honey, and lemon juice to form a paste. Smooth the paste over your face and leave on for 15 minutes. Rinse off with lukewarm water. Apply a refreshing astringent (see next recipe).

Refreshing Astringent

1 tbsp. witch hazel
1 1/2 cups distilled water
2 tsp. salt
1/4 tsp. oil of wintergreen

Dissolve salt in distilled water. Add other ingredients. Put in a clean bottle and warm it under hot running water. Shake to blend ingredients each time before using. Apply with cotton balls and let dry. This can be refrigerated for use on a hot day.

2. Plan and schedule a routine to care for your skin and hair. How often do you shampoo, condition, cut your hair? What is your skin type and how can you take care of it? Learn about the different products suitable for your hair and skin type; then comparison shop for quality and price.

3. Have an "experiment with color and accessories" party! Collect sizable pieces of fabric in different colors, and have everybody bring in their used but good accessories (belts, jewelry, hats, scarves, headbands, and other hair accessories) that they would like to trade in. Take turns holding the fabric up to your face. Decide which color family looks best on you: the cool family (lavenders and plums), the warm family (corals, pinks, and reds), or the neutral family (beiges and peaches). Then, experiment with items from the accessory pool. How many different looks can you create? Have an accessory exchange to recycle pieces.

4. In place of the traditional pajama party, hold a "looking your best retreat." Give each other manicures and pedicures, set each other's hair, try on makeup, and create natural beauty treatments. Try soaking fingernails in warm olive oil for 10 minutes before your manicure. Massage feet and hands with baby oil. Put on cotton socks and gloves for an overnight beauty treatment. For refreshments prepare a simple meal of natural foods such as pasta, salad, and fruit.

5. Experiment with different hair styles. Try something new like bangs or a side part. Have your hair braided in elaborate styles, perhaps with ribbons or other ornaments braided in. Solicit someone from the neighborhood or school, perhaps a professional hair stylist or another girl who can help the group.

6. Be a wise health care consumer. Collect several magazine advertisements for each of the following products: deodorant, anti-perspirant, skin care products (soaps, cleansers, toners, astringents), shampoos, conditioners, and lotions. Compare them according to their claims, labels, ingredients, reputations, and so forth. Discuss which ones you would be tempted to try and why.

7. Rank the following grooming and health products and services in the order of their importance to you today. Then rank them according to how important you think they will be to you in 20 years. Discuss the reasons behind your choices:

Product or Service	Importance	
	Today	In 20 Years
Acne medication		
Doctor appointment		
Deodorant		
Cold medicine		
Perfume		
Gym shoes		
A low-sodium diet		
Pain relievers		
Makeup		
Products with oat bran		
A stationary bicycle		
Hand weights		

8. Drink plenty of water, at least six to ten glasses daily, to hydrate the skin from inside out. Fill up a half-gallon container of water and drink from it when you get home until bedtime. Place a tall glass of water next to you as you study. Perk it up! Try the following recipe:

Sparkling Flavored Water

1 tall glass sparkling mineral or seltzer water
1 tsp. vanilla extract
1 tsp. sugar or artificial sweetener

Mix together for a refreshing drink. Substitute different extracts of your choice for variety. Add pieces of fruit for an additional treat.

9. Invite a doctor or health care worker to talk about establishing a good grooming and personal hygiene routine. Use the library to help you select audiovisuals on the topic to view and discuss as a group.

10. Society changes its idea of beauty over the years. What you consider beautiful today, may not be the standard of beauty years ago. The standard of beauty may also be different in different cultures or countries. Interview women and men of different ages, and if possible, from different cultural or ethnic backgrounds. Ask them what the standard of beauty was or is in their culture. For older women and especially for those from different countries, ask them how the standard of beauty was different years ago. Write down what you have learned, and report back to the total group to compare notes.

11. Make a list of successful, respected people who do not fit the perfect standard of beauty; perhaps they are overweight or have wrinkles or an extra-large nose. Also, look through fashion and beauty magazines to find realistic and unrealistic examples of beauty. An unrealistic example of beauty is something unattainable in a natural way by most people. Notice that many beauty make-overs enhance the person's looks in a realistic way.

12. Cut out several magazine pictures of people who look like your "ideal" person. Base your ideal on the person's physical attributes, size, hair/eye coloring, age, clothes, or overall appearance. Display all pictures on a bulletin board or attach them to cardboard backing. View all pictures; then discuss your individual selections and the group's general findings. Explain why these pictures represent your ideal, and as a group, discuss what all the pictures have in common and how they differ.

13. Write and illustrate a good grooming booklet for younger girls. Determine what topics or chapters should be included. Divide them up among the group so that two or three girls can work on each chapter.

14. Collect a number of advertisements from different sources, especially from magazines. Rate the advertisement on each of the following factors. Use this scale:

SA = Strongly agree   D = Disagree
A = Agree   SD = Strongly disagree
U = Undecided   NA = Not applicable

Give the name and a brief description of the advertised product. Which of the following statements apply to the advertisement that you selected?

1. Associates the use of the product with being attractive.

2. Associates the use of the product with fun.

3. Suggests that use of the product will result in a positive body image.

4. Shows the model using the product.

5. Suggests that using the product will improve physical or intellectual performance.

6. Suggests that using the product will make one popular or have plenty of friends.

7. Encourages the opinion that everybody else uses the product.

Write your personal evaluation of the advertisement. What audience do you think it is aimed at? How does the ad encourage the audience to buy its product?

15. In groups of two or three depending upon the size of the troop, find out what you can about at least two of the following medical specialists.

allergist	obstetrician
anesthesiologist	ophthalmologist
cardiologist	pediatrician
dermatologist	plastic surgeon
gynecologist	podiatrist
hematologist	psychiatrist
neurologist	radiologist

List each specialist on a piece of paper; fold it up, and draw it from a hat. Only your group should know which specialists you have. After each group has gathered information about its medical specialists, the total troop will come together for a game of charades. Each group must act out one or more of its medical specialties. The other groups have three minutes to correctly name the specialty. Note: to make the game a little easier, everyone can be given the total list of medical specialists.

16. For young Girl Scouts, create a picture story that gives the reader a good health message. Find pictures for most of the words in the following message. Then, decide on a message of your own to use as a picture story.

"I wash my hands before I eat."

"I brush my teeth every morning and before I go to bed."

17. Invite a dentist or dental hygienist to talk to girls about proper care of their teeth. They should learn how to brush and floss teeth effectively, and how to select the right toothbrush and toothpaste.

18. Another professional health care worker can talk to older girls about the importance of breast self-examinations.

BIBLIOGRAPHY

Brumberg, Joan Jacobs, *Fasting Girls: The History of Anorexia Nervosa* (New York: New American Library, 1989).

Garzino, Mary S., *Into Adolescence: Fitness, Health and Hygiene*. A curriculum for grades 5–8 (Santa Cruz, Calif.: Network Publications, 1991). P.O. Box 1830, Santa Cruz, Calif. 95061-1830.

Giarratano, Susan, *Entering Adulthood: Looking at Body Image and Eating Disorders*. A curriculum for Grades 9–12 (Santa Cruz, Calif.: Network Publications, 1991).

Girl Scouts of the U.S.A., *Girls Are Great: Growing Up Female*. Contemporary Issues booklet (New York: GSUSA, 1987).

Heit, Philip, and Linda Meeks, *Comprehensive School Health Education* (Blacklick, Ohio: MeeksHeit Publishing Co., 1992). P.O. Box 121, Blacklick, Ohio 43004.

Hisgen, Jon W., *Into Adolescence: Becoming a Health-Wise Consumer*. A curriculum for grades 5–8 (Santa Cruz, Calif.: Network Publications, 1990).

Lasch, Judith, *Faces: For Teens, a Step-by-Step Guide to Healthy Skin and Great Make-up*. Videotape running time: 45 minutes (New York: Lasch Media Productions, 1991). 50 Tindall Road, Suite 101, Middletown, N.J. 07748. 908-671-3191.

Luetje, Carolyn, and Carol Quinn, *Happy, Healthy and Fit! Whole Health Activities for Children Ages 4–8* (West Nyack, N.Y.: 1992), Center for Applied Research in Education, West Nyack, N.Y. 10995.

Schwab, Anne, *Get Yourself Together: The Fashion Guide for Teens!* (Reston, Va.: Acropolis Books Ltd., 1987).

Tillman, Kenneth G., and Patricia Rizzo Toner, *How to Survive Teaching Health, Games, Activities, and Worksheets*. For grades 4–12 (West Nyack, N.Y.: 1990). Parker Publishing Co., West Nyack, N.Y. 10995.

Swift, David, and Kathleen Zraly, *Anorexia, Bulimia and Compulsive Overeating: A Practical Guide for Counselors and Families* (New York: Continuum Press, 1990).

Chapter 6

ENVIRONMENTAL FACTORS, THE SIXTH COMPONENT OF A HEALTH AND FITNESS PLAN

Environment is defined as the conditions that surround an organism. In this chapter, we will look at how we, as organisms, are affected by our surroundings, and what we can do to help ensure a healthy environment.

Women and children have been referred to as the "canaries" of environmental problems. Canaries used to be kept in coal mines to monitor air quality. If the bird keeled over, it was time to evacuate because the air was bad. Women are often the first to notice environmental conditions that affect food sources, reproduction, and children. Illness and birth defects are often caused by an unhealthy environment. Children are usually the first to show the effects of repeated exposure to toxic conditions, such as lead poisoning or chemicals in food or air.

We all interact with our environment, wherever we may be. Much of our environment has been affected by human development. Because of this, we now test air, water, and soil to find out if they are polluted. Everything is connected. If water is polluted, the fish we use for food from the water can be polluted as well. As we work to stop such pollution, we also work to restore parts of our environment to a healthy state.

As individuals, we can make decisions about the foods we eat, the air we breathe, the places we live, and the kinds of products we buy. We can also choose to live in ways that minimize our impact on the environment. Water conservation, recycling, and conserving energy are all such choices. These are choices made in the present that take into account our future generations and their right to a healthy environment. These choices are also important in role modeling for girls we work with.

Our individual decisions are connected to our community, our nation, and our global environment. It takes a lot of people working together to conserve water or to reduce the amount of garbage being taken to a regional landfill. Likewise, it takes many countries working together to reduce the amount of chemicals that are being released into the atmosphere, destroying the ozone layer.

43

In order to make decisions about environmental health, knowledge is essential. For ourselves and the girls we work with:

■ We need to be aware of problems in order to address them.

■ We need to be able to gather factual information about environmental problems.

■ We must understand related issues that can help to shape solutions.

■ We must develop evaluation skills to assist in decision-making and deal with misinformation, lack of research, economic competition, and vested interests. Advertising and interest groups often affect information available to the public.

Where can we start on the trail to knowledge, particularly if we are acting as a resource for girls? Many, but not all, of the environmental issues are introduced in GSUSA's *Earth Matters: A Challenge for Environmental Action*. The book, along with the bibliography in this chapter, is constructed to assist both adults and girls in examining issues and learning about the environment. It is important to look at more than one resource and more than one side of an issue before making decisions. Look for resource people in your community. Your local library or bookstore will also carry many books and magazines that address environmental health.

As an adult it is important to separate your own value judgments from issues when letting girls explore aspects of environmental health. Girls will come with values from peers, family, and society. As a leader, you can help them explore the reasons for some of their feelings and beliefs, collect information, and make observations. Help them to realize the connection between the health of the environment and their own personal health. Explore ways that they can create a healthier environment. Clean air, clean water, and a pollution-free environment are basic human rights. We must be concerned for our health and fitness when the environment we live in is not healthy.

The following are specific environmental concerns that are likely to affect us and the girls we work with, and some ways of approaching them from a health and fitness perspective.

WEATHER

When we think of weather, we usually think of heat or cold, rain or sun. In terms of health and fitness, we need to take into consideration the proper clothing for the environment we are a part of, as well as being prepared for changing conditions. Being in good health is important preparation for surviving in inclement weather, whether it is freezing cold or very hot. Common sense is also part of the picture. Knowing when to come in out of the rain, when to cool down, when to drink hot or cold liquids, or learning first aid are all a part of preparing for the climate presented us. Don't forget the man-made environment as well. Exercising in a closed room without ventilation, having too many layers for the indoors, and neglecting to drink water indoors can also negatively affect health.

■ Make a clothing review part of your safety plan. Discuss what to wear for each activity. Use Girl Scout age-level books as a resource for discussions on what to wear.

■ Dress in layers for maximum protection and flexibility.

■ Learn what materials are the best for warm weather or cold weather.

■ Know basic first aid for sunburn, heat stroke, and heat exhaustion before taking your group outdoors for physical exercise in the sun. Learn how to recognize and treat cold weather problems such as hypothermia and frostbite as well.

■ Always make sure girls are wearing sunscreen and sun hats when out under the sun.

■ Be flexible when severe inclement weather is on the horizon. Do not get locked into going somewhere if the weather conditions are apt to catch you unprepared. Exercise your veto power as an adult and help the girls understand why.

WATER QUALITY

Having good, fresh, uncontaminated water is essential to our survival. Many people around the world, particularly children, die each year from waterborne diseases. Many more die from drought. Chemicals and ground water contaminants have been responsible for birth defects and deaths. Is it any wonder that water quality often heads the list when we speak of environmental health?

Water pollution affects the air we breathe and the food we eat. Pollution of the oceans, which cover almost 75 percent of our planet, affects plankton, microscopic plants that produce much of the earth's oxygen. Acid rain, caused by pollutants emitted from automobiles and factories that have mixed with water in the atmosphere, is responsible for the death of many freshwater lakes. The acidity kills algae and oxygen-producing plants, as well as fish living in the lakes. Acid rain is also responsible for the deaths of many forests, particularly in the Northern Hemisphere.

In all Girl Scout activities, we are concerned with water quality, whether it is making sure that the water we drink is safe, or practicing minimal-impact camping around water resources. We also advocate water conservation in our activities and facilities. Here are some guidelines:

■ When exercising or involved in outdoor recreational activities, make sure that fresh water is available, whether it is from a faucet or carried by girls in water bottles.

■ Carry and use water-purifying or filtration kits when traveling in back-country areas.

■ Dispose of all wastes away from water sources.

■ Do not dump chemicals or toxins into water-waste systems.

■ Water used for recreational purposes must meet health department and *Safety-Wise* standards.

■ Consult the local health department or the U.S. Environmental Protection Agency for questions on water quality in your area.

■ Practice good water conservation by such actions as recycling of gray water, limiting showers, installing water monitors on showers, and keeping pipes and faucets maintained to eliminate leaks.

AIR QUALITY

The air we breathe is shared by every living creature on this planet. Green plants use carbon dioxide and sunlight to manufacture oxygen, a cycle that is basic to all life. Yet we are rapidly losing natural areas to development; rain forests of the world are being lost to logging and agriculture; and industrialization is adding chemicals and gases to the atmosphere. As a result, the cycle shows signs of stress.

Natural and industrial disasters, such as volcanic eruptions and nuclear power plant accidents, have been felt globally due to airborne particles. Air pollution has been responsible for the death of crops and forests.

An additional concern is the changing ozone levels in the atmosphere. In the upper atmosphere, the ozone layer protects plants and animals by filtering harmful ultraviolet radiation from the sun. Exposure to ultraviolet rays can cause sunburn, skin cancer, and cataracts in mammals, as well as damage to plant life. Holes are appearing in this upper layer of ozone, caused by chlorofluorocarbons, or CFCs. These are chemicals used in air conditioners, refrigerators, fire extinguishers, and some cleaning solvents. Closer to earth, excessive ozone is being produced in chemical reactions between sunlight and the chemicals created from the burning of fossil fuels, particularly car exhaust. This ozone in the air we breathe causes lung damage and weakened immune systems.

Poor air quality has led to an increase in respiratory illness, particularly among children and the elderly. It has led to "air quality alerts" in many of our cities, and some laws to cut down on air pollution by automobiles and factory emissions.

In any activity, air quality can become an issue when working with girls.

■ Make sure that any indoor meeting area is well ventilated.

■ Ensure a smoke-free environment for girls. Do not meet in an area where smoking is allowed, and ask all smokers to abstain when around the girls, particularly in indoor and eating areas.

■ Walk, bicycle, use public transportation to avoid overuse of the automobile. Car pool or use public transportation whenever planning field trips.

■ Know which children have allergies to air-borne particles, and make sure that those with asthma have medication or inhalers at all times.

■ Know first aid for sunburn, starting with prevention. Girls should use sunscreen and wear hats and long-sleeved shirts when out for long periods of time. No matter how dark a person's skin is, it can be damaged by the sun.

■ Avoid practices that add CFCs to the atmosphere. That is, avoid products that contain CFCs such as some cleaning solutions and some types of fire extinguishers.

■ Avoid strenuous activity on days with air quality warnings. Monitor the conditions prior to events and activities.

■ Wear protective eye-wear when exercising or involved in recreational activities in sunny or windy conditions. It is important to protect eyes against the ultraviolet rays of the sun.

NOISE POLLUTION

The sense of hearing allows us to experience our environment in a less tangible way. The sound of ocean waves breaking on the shore, or the wind in the trees can calm us, while the crack of thunder or the roar of an avalanche can warn us against danger. With the sophistication of sound reproduction and sound amplification, we now have more experiences with loud sounds. Hearing loss due to extended exposures to loud sounds, such as rock music, has increased dramatically. In industry and on the job, workers are required by law to protect their ears. Young people at concerts or plugged into their earphones listening to rock music have no such protection.

Noise pollution can take many other forms. We get used to certain levels of sound, such as traffic and crowds, and do not realize the tension created by those sounds until removed from them. There are ways to measure the levels of sound, and recommended levels of sound. Many communities have noise level laws, which are often difficult to enforce.

It is important for girls to realize that sound is something that they can control, whether by choos-ing to wear ear protection or by turning down the sound on their radios. Some tips are:

■ Use protective ear gear whenever using heavy machinery. If something like a power saw is being used around a group, develop signals to use and assign spotters.

■ Have the group establish noise level guidelines for meetings and activities. Use a quiet signal that the girls all recognize.

■ Always check to see where people are before blowing a whistle to call the group together. Whistles blown in confined spaces or near someone's ear can cause damage.

OTHER THINGS THAT ARE HARMFUL IN THE ENVIRONMENT

In looking at water and air quality we have addressed concerns regarding pollutants, and have seen how air and water often are carriers of contamination. Add to this a concern about the land itself, and growing things which are a part of our diet. Waterborne chemicals can contaminate soil. Erosion or mining of natural minerals from the soil can contaminate water or agricultural lands. Plants absorb these chemicals or minerals, and they are eaten by animals and people.

Insecticides, growth hormones, medications, and other chemicals used to create better crops or healthier animals become a part of us if we eat the crops or animals. Additives and preservatives that are used to increase the shelf life of products become a part of us. While not all such chemicals are harmful to people in the quantities that finally reach them, there are an increasing number of people who have developed allergies to such additives. Children, because their bodies are still developing, are much more susceptible to illnesses and allergies from chemical additives.

Many manufactured products cause allergic reactions—plastics, perfumes, carpeting, packaging, beauty products, to name a few.

The natural environment also contains many things that can be health concerns. There are local plants and animals, including insects and reptiles, that can cause allergic reactions and even death.

Wild animals and insects can carry diseases that are harmful to people, such as rabies or Lyme disease. As an adult working with girls, your concern must always be for their health and safety.

Field trips and menu planning can become opportunities to explore environmental health issues. Knowledge about potential environmental hazards is part of any safety plan, along with training in basic first aid. The following suggestions can help you become more knowledgeable about your environment and learn about precautions that can make your outdoor time safer:

■ Learn the environmental history of your neighborhood, community, and such places as parks and recreation sites. Are there histories of dumping, industrial development, or ground-water contamination? Check with your local health department.

■ Learn about poisonous plants and animals that are native to your area. This includes snakes and insects.

■ Learn first aid for bee stings, insect bites, poison oak or poison ivy, stinging nettles, jellyfish stings, and other natural environmental hazards.

■ Find out if Lyme disease, carried by deer ticks, is a concern in your area. If so, wear recommended long pants, socks, and long-sleeve shirt, as well as taping sock and pants together. Use an insect repellent containing DEET on clothes. Check for ticks after being outdoors.

■ Rocky Mountain spotted fever, bubonic plague, and rabies are all diseases that can be transmitted by contact with an insect or animal. Contact the state or local health department prior to back-country hiking.

■ Follow guidelines in *Safety-Wise* and *Girl Scout Camping Guidelines* for food handling and storage.

■ Learn where your foods come from. Where are your fresh vegetables and fruits grown? Decide whether you want to buy food that has been chemically treated. Visit a store that sells food that has not been chemically treated. Compare fruits and vegetables that have and have not been treated. Show what you value through your purchasing.

■ When doing group events, find out whether sufficient refrigeration is available. Foods such as meats, mayonnaise, or eggs spoil easily when not refrigerated, unless they can be added or mixed immediately prior to serving.

■ Know what food and chemical allergies your girls have, and be prepared to deal with them. If a girl is allergic to bee stings, she should always have her bee sting kit or medication with her on outings.

ACTIVITIES FOR GIRLS

■ Make up a game that involves different weather conditions and the best clothing to wear. For example: Make different-colored cards for types of weather (cold rain, snow, mild, hot, windy) and parts of the body (feet, lower body, upper body, head, skin). A player must draw a weather card followed by a body part card. She has five seconds to name an appropriate article of clothing for the body part.

■ Make up a play that talks about how to protect yourself from the sun. Include the following facts:

● Sunlight is strongest between 11 A.M. and 3 P.M.
● You can sunburn on hazy or cloudy days because of the ultraviolet rays.
● You should wear a waterproof sunblock with at least a #15 sun protection factor (SPF 15).
● Wear a sun hat to protect your head, but watch out for reflection from water or bright surfaces.
● You sunburn faster at high altitudes (there is less atmosphere to protect you from ultraviolet rays) and on water or snow (due to the sun's reflection).
● Wear sunglasses to protect from glare and ultraviolet rays. Never look directly at the sun.
● Always have a long-sleeve shirt to protect yourself.

■ A food chain is the passage of food and energy from a green plant to a plant-eating animal to a meat-eating animal. Draw a simple food chain, with yourself being the last link. Discuss reasons for eating "low on the food chain" in terms of energy conservation and effects on the environment. Make up a menu that has you eating low on the food chain. Visit a health food store and a supermarket and compare the costs of the food for your menu.

■ Learn to purify water at least one way. You might use a water filter, a solar oven, a solar still, or a water-purifying chemical.

■ Learn how water in a swimming pool is tested to determine if it is safe. Learn how to collect water to test for chemical or fecal contamination by visiting your health department.

■ Find out if your area is affected by acid rain. Use litmus paper or a simple water test kit to determine if water is acidic.

■ For two weeks, collect articles from newspapers or magazines that are about environmental health issues. Discuss these issues with another person or your troop or group. Decide on an action that you could take that can affect one of the issues you have discussed.

■ Visit your local health department. Find out what jobs are associated with environmental and public health. Find out what local environmental health issues your health department is most concerned about.

■ Some plants act as natural air filters. Find out what plants are best for keeping indoors to help purify air. Grow an indoor plant from seed, cutting, or rootstock and learn to care for it.

■ Find out how air purifiers work and price them. Determine which would best fit your family's needs.

■ Visit a store that carries makeup and cosmetics. Evaluate product packaging in terms of environmental impact. Is there excess packaging? Are the packaging materials easy to recycle? Are the contents biodegradable? Compare products and find out how much you are paying for packaging. Look for products that advertise themselves as environmentally safe. How do they differ? Are they more or less costly?

■ Do some research, using a magazine like *Consumer Reports*, *Zillions*, or *Garbage*, or current books from your local library to find out what factors are considered when certifying a product environmentally safe. Find out what kinds of "green labeling" are available in your community, and who makes the decisions about whether a product is "green" (environmentally safe). Make a list of health care and food products that you would consider "green" and choose one to make an advertisement about, selling it as a "green" product. Share your advertisement with your troop or group.

■ Explore how different colors affect you. Find out if there are colors that are soothing, energizing, exciting, depressing to you. Find out what colors decorators use for different types of rooms or what colors people wear to change their own moods.

■ Plan an environmental action project that combines health and caring for the environment. (Refer to *Earth Matters: A Challenge for Environmental Action*, cited in the bibliography.) This could be something that cleans up your community, creates a place to exercise or enjoy nature, or creates public awareness about a health issue, such as clean water.

■ Find out what environmental laws or ordinances affect your community in relation to water, garbage, noise, and other health issues. Are there any additional laws or ordinances that you feel your community needs?

■ In many parts of the country, ticks are a problem for people who have outdoor forms of recreation. Find out how to prevent diseases carried by ticks, such as Lyme disease or Rocky Mountain spotted fever. Put on a fashion show or skit for your group, your troop, or another troop to show how to dress to avoid ticks. Learn what to do if you find a tick, and how to recognize symptoms of these diseases.

■ Find out what the acceptable noise levels are

in your community. Use a machine to measure decibel levels on the street, in a group meeting, at a concert, and so forth.

■ Determine what kinds of noises are soothing and what kinds of noises put you on edge. Keep a record of how sound affects you for a week.

■ Learn about poisonous plants and animals in your environment. Learn how to recognize them and how to give first aid if a person is bitten, stung, or ingests something that is poisonous.

■ Determine how to buy fresh food. This includes meat, fish, fruit, and vegetables. Visit a supermarket or open air market and compare food quality. Make a list of practices to avoid in handling, preparing, and storing food. Look at the guidelines in *Safety-Wise* concerning food handling and food storage.

■ Find out if radon (a natural radioactive gas) is a problem in your community. If so, use a radon test kit to test for radon in your troop or group meeting place (unless tests have already been made).

■ When planning a recreational event, make a list of minimal impact activities that you can include as part of your event, such as recycling drink cans, using public transportation or car pooling, having people bring their own cups, or picking up litter. Involve all the participants.

■ Keep track of your daily travels for a week. How many times do you walk, ride your bicycle, ride public transportation, or ride in a car? Are there ways that you can increase the exercise you are getting by walking or bicycling more? Are there ways you can get more errands done in one car trip, or use public transportation to cut down on energy use? Share your findings with your family and your troop or group.

BIBLIOGRAPHY

American Heart Association, "We're Fighting for Your Life." Series of health care brochures. American Heart Association, National Center, 7320 Greenville Avenue, Dallas, Tex. 75231.

Caduto, Michael J., and Joseph Bruchac, *Keepers of the Earth: Native American Stories and Environmental Activities for Children* (Golden, Colo.: Fulcrum, Inc., 1988).

Corson, Walter H., ed., *Citizen's Guide to Sustainable Development* (Washington, D.C.: Global Tomorrow Coalition, 1990). 1325 G Street N.W., Suite 915, Washington, D.C. 20005-3104.

Dadd, Debra Lynn, *Nontoxic and Natural: A Guide for Consumers* (Los Angeles, Calif.: Jeremy P. Tarcher, 1984).

Girl Scouts of the U.S.A., *Earth Matters: A Challenge for Environmental Action.* Contemporary Issues booklet (New York: GSUSA, 1990).

Harris, D. Mark, *Embracing the Earth: Choices for Environmentally Sound Living* (Chicago: Noble Press, 1990).

Java, John, *50 Simple Things Kids Can Do to Save the Earth* (Kansas City, Mo.: Andrews and McMeel, 1990).

Lewis, Barbara, *The Kid's Guide to Social Action* (Minneapolis: Free Spirit Publishing, 1991). Suite 616, 400 First Avenue North, Minneapolis, Minn. 55401-1724.

Miles, Betty, *Save the Earth! An Ecology Handbook for Kids* (New York: Alfred A. Knopf, 1974).

GLOSSARY

aerobic (with oxygen): the ability of the lungs and heart to use oxygen more efficiently.

aerobic exercise: activity that is steady and at a pace where the heart can supply as much oxygen as the body needs.

biodegradable: capable of being decomposed by natural, biological processes.

calisthenics: a series of athletic exercises performed by a person; simple gymnastics.

cardiovascular fitness: ability of the heart, lungs, and circulatory system to supply the nutrients necessary for an extended period of work or exercise.

cholesterol: a waxlike substance found in animal food products that can clog up the blood vessels and arteries.

coordination: all of the parts working together as a whole.

cross training: using two or more sports or activities to obtain a desired level of fitness.

dandruff: an infection of the scalp that causes the scalp cells to come off in flakes.

dehydration: excessive water loss from the body.

endurance: the ability to withstand the stress of physical exercise over a period of time.

fiber: the natural bulk of plant food. When eaten, it enables sugar to be released more slowly and evenly into the bloodstream, aids digestion, and helps protect against heart disease.

fitness: the ability of the whole body, through vigorous effort, to function at optimum efficiency.

flexibility: the ability to move legs, arms, or other body parts easily through their range of motion; the ability to stretch muscles without pain.

health: your body and mind being without sickness or injury—being sound in body and mind.

lifestyle: how one lives on a daily basis—one's whole way of living.

maximum heart rate: the rate of heartbeat that you should not go beyond when exercising.

melanoma: a skin cancer usually caused by overexposure to the sun's harmful ultraviolet rays.

metabolism: how our bodies use the foods we eat; all of the chemical and biological changes that take place in the body.

muscular strength: the degree of power or force that muscles are able to exert at one time.

nutrition: the body's process of assimilating food and using it for growth and replacement of tissues.

obesity: being fat—having too many fat cells stored in the body.

osteoporosis: a bone loss disease that primarily affects older women.

ozone: the gaseous layer of the earth's atmosphere that blocks out the harmful ultraviolet rays of the sun.

passive smoking: the inhalation of smoke produced by another person's cigarette; secondhand smoking.

pollution: the contamination of the earth, water, or air by harmful substances.

recovery rate: the amount of time the body takes to regain its normal condition after exercise.

relaxation: a reduction of stress, calming of body and mind.

resting heart rate: the heart rate while the body is resting.

smog: a combination of "smoke" and "fog"; air pollution consisting of carbon monoxide, soot, sulfur, and other ingredients.

SPF (sun protection factor): A number such as 15 means the product will protect the skin from harmful sun rays fifteen times more than if the skin were left unprotected.

stamina: endurance, the ability to practice over a long period of time, the ability to resist fatigue.

stress: force, pressure, or strain placed on the body or mind. Ways we make ourselves tense or less tense.

target heart rate: the range of heart rate that will give the individual the greatest cardiovascular benefits.

weight control: the ability to bring or maintain one's body weight within prescribed limits.

RESOURCES

Consultants: physical education teacher, nutritionist, dietitian, family doctor, nurse, exercise physiologist, yoga instructor, behavior therapist, sports medicine physician, physical therapist, chiropractor, fitness consultant, health education teachers.

Local groups: schools, wellness clinics, women's health clinics, exercise clubs, swim clubs, hospitals, local schools and varsity teams, martial arts schools, stress clinics, diet groups, sports medicine clinics, mental health clinics, self-help groups, other youth agencies.

NATIONAL ORGANIZATIONS

American Academy of Pediatrics
141 Northwest Point Boulevard
P.O. Box 927
Elk Grove Village, Ill. 60009

American Association of University Women
1111 Sixteenth Street, N.W.
Washington, D.C. 20036-4873

American Fitness Association
820 Hillside Drive
Long Beach, Calif. 90815

American Heart Association
7320 Greenville Avenue
Dallas, Tex. 75231

American Medical Association
515 North State Street
Chicago, Ill. 60610

American Yoga Association
3130 Mayfield Road, W-103
Cleveland Heights, Ohio 44118

Association for Advancement in Health
1900 Association Drive
Reston, Va. 22091

Children's Defense Fund
25 East Street, N.W.
Washington, D.C. 20001

Creative Walking Inc.
P.O. Box 50296
Clayton, Mo. 63105

Fitness Involving Teen and Youth with Disabilities
   (Project FIT)
P.O. Box 1781
Longview, Wash. 98632

Jump Rope for Heart Event Kit
American Heart Association
National Center
7320 Greenville Avenue
Dallas, Tex. 75231

Melpomene Institute
1010 University Avenue
St. Paul, Minn. 55104

National Association for Girls and Women in Sports
1900 Association Drive
Reston, Va. 22091

National Dairy Council
10255 West Higgins Road
Rosemont, Ill. 60018-5616

National Fitness Foundation
17992 Mitchell S100
Irvine, Calif. 92714-6813

National Health Information Clearinghouse
P.O. Box 1133
Washington, D.C. 20013-1133

National Mental Health Association
1021 Prince Street
Alexandria, Va. 22314-2971

National Strength and Conditioning Association
P.O. Box 81410
Lincoln, Nebr. 68501

National Women's Health Network
1325 G Street, N.W.
Washington, D.C. 20005

President's Council on Physical Fitness and Sports
Suite 250
701 Pennsylvania Avenue, N.W.
Washington, D.C. 20005

Roller Skating Rink Operators Association
7700 A Street
Lincoln, Nebr. 68501

Search Institute
122 West Franklin Avenue, Suite 525
Minneapolis, Minn. 55404

Tambrands, Inc.
777 Westchester Avenue
White Plains, N.Y. 10604

U.S. Taekwondo Union
1750 East Boulder Street, Suite 404
Colorado Springs, Colo. 80909

Women's Sports Foundation
Eisenhower Park
East Meadow, N.Y. 11554

SPECIAL PROGRAMS

Physical Best
American Alliance for Health, Physical Education,
   Recreation, and Dance
1900 Association Drive
Reston, Va. 22091

Presidential Sports Award
P.O. Box 5214
FDR Post Office
New York, N.Y. 10022

Project Go-For-Health
Dr. Guy Parcel, Director
Center for Health Promotion Research and
   Development
School of Public Health
P.O. Box 2018
University of Texas Health Science Center
Houston, Tex. 77225

ABOUT KIDS AND SAFETY

Heart Smart Program
National Research and Demonstration Center
L.S.U. Medical Center
1542 Tulane Avenue
New Orleans, La. 70112-2822

Heart Treasure Chest
American Heart Association, National Center
7320 Greenville Avenue
Dallas, Tex. 75231
(Or local AHA affiliate)

National Coalition to Prevent Childhood Injury
111 Michigan Avenue, N.W.
Washington, D.C. 20010-2970

National Council for Research on Women
Sara Delano Roosevelt Memorial House
47-49 East 65th Street
New York, N.Y. 10021

Sun Flower Project
Shawnee Mission
Instructional Program Center
6649 Lamar
Shawnee Mission, Kans. 66202

NOTES

NOTES